Praise for **DAVID RABE** and *THE BLACK MONK*

"Rabe's theatrical universe is at once vivid and mysterious, a pageant and a puzzle, where his bemused characters glimpse only the barest outline of . . . 'the unrelenting havoc' in which they flounder . . . [His] daringly stylized dramas hover in the realms between the natural and the metaphorical . . . Rabe is expert at building the awful pressure of impending woe."
—JOHN LAHR, *THE NEW YORKER*

"*The Black Monk* is a great play. . . . Mr. Rabe has heightened theatrical possibilities by extending descriptive passages into dramatic scenes that catch fire . . . a heady event."
—ALVIN KLEIN, *THE NEW YORK TIMES*

The Black Monk has been called a singular "collaboration" between two writers: Anton Chekhov and David Rabe. Based on Chekhov's novella of the same name, Rabe's brilliant stage adaptation tells the story of Kovrin, the young philosophy student who returns from Moscow to the estate owned by Pesotsky, where he spent his youth. Kovrin and Pesotsky's daughter, Tanya, soon fall in love and plan to marry. But the appearance of an emissary from the unknown—the black monk—threatens to have a devastating effect on them.

Vastly different in their aesthetic, these two highly praised plays embody all of the celebrated hallmarks of David Rabe's writing and art: unflinchingly honest and perceptive themes, starkly luminous dialogue, and the unsettling humor which have made him an icon of the American theater for more than forty years.

DAVID RABE is the author of many widely performed plays, including *The Basic Training of Pavlo Hummel, Sticks and Bones, In the Boom Boom Room, Streamers, Hurlyburly*, and *The Dog Problem*. Four of his plays have been nominated for the Tony Award, including a win for Best Play. He is the recipient of an Obie Award, the American Academy of Arts and Letters Award, Drama Desk Award, and the New York Drama Critics Circle Award, among others. His numerous screenwriting credits include *I'm Dancing As Fast As I Can, Casualties of War, Hurlyburly,* and *The Firm.* Rabe is the critically acclaimed author of the novels *Dinosaurs on the Roof* and *Recital of the Dog,* and a collection of short stories, *A Primitive Heart.* Born in Dubuque, Iowa, Rabe lives with his family in northwest Connecticut.

ALSO BY DAVID RABE

Plays
Cosmologies
A Question of Mercy
(based on the diary of Richard Selzer)
Those the River Keeps
Hurlyburly
Goose and Tomtom
In the Boom Boom Room

The Vietnam Plays
Streamers
The Orphan
Sticks and Bones
The Basic Training of Pavlo Hummel

Fiction
Dinosaurs on the Roof
A Primitive Heart
Recital of the Dog

Children's Books
Mr. Wellington

the black monk

David Rabe

SIMON & SCHUSTER PAPERBACKS
New York   London   Toronto   Sydney

Simon & Schuster
1230 Avenue of the Americas
New York, NY 10020

First Simon & Schuster trade paperback edition July 2009

SIMON & SCHUSTER and colophon are registered trademarks
of Simon & Schuster, Inc.

For information about special discounts for bulk purchases,
please contact Simon & Schuster Special Sales at 1-866-506-1949
or business@simonandschuster.com.

The Simon & Schuster Speakers Bureau can bring authors to your live event.
For more information or to book an event contact the Simon & Schuster
Speakers Bureau at 1-866-248-3049 or visit our website at
www.simonspeakers.com.

Designed by Jaime Putorti

Manufactured in the United States of America

10 9 8 7 6 5 4 3 2 1

Library of Congress Cataloging-in-Publication Data

Rabe, David.
    The black monk ; and, The dog problem : two plays / David Rabe.
       p. cm.
    I. Rabe, David. Dog problem. II. Title.
PS3568.A23B53 2009
812'.54—dc22

                                                              2009017588

ISBN 978-1-4391-4188-5 (trade pbk.)

*For Marsha, my sister
and first scene partner*

CAST FROM ORIGINAL PRODUCTION

Principals (in order of appearance)

YEGOR SEMYONITCH PESOTSKY.....................Sam Waterston
TANYA ....Jenny Bacon
ORLOV .... Leo Leyden
ANDREI VASILICH KOVRIN............................Thomas Jay Ryan
THE BLACK MONK..................................... Christopher McCann
VARVARA NIKOLAEVNA ....Pamela Nyberg

Ensemble

NADIA .... Nancy Anderson
MIKHAIL...Paul Mullins
YAKOV .... Haynes Thigpen

OTHER BLACK MONKS, CONCIERGE,
BELLMAN, WORKERS................ Nancy Anderson, Paul Mullins,
Haynes Thigpen, Mathew Martin, Jeffery Withers.

The Yale Repertory Theatre (James Bundy, Artistic Director; Victoria Nolan, Managing Director; Mark Bly, Associate Artistic Director) in New Haven, Connecticut on May 9, 2003. Directed by Daniel Fish; scenic design by Christine Jones; costume design by Jane Greenwood; lighting design by Stephen Strawbridge; music and sound design by Leah Gelpe; stage manager, Karen Quisenberry.

The text of this edition of *The Black Monk* was revised in cooperation with The Undermain Theatre production that opened in Dallas, Texas, on April 4, 2009.

Principals (in order of appearance)

YEGOR SEMYONITCH PESOTSKY	Bruce DuBose
TANYA	Shannon Kearns-Simmons
ORLOV	Richard Rollin
ANDREI VASILICH KOVRIN	Jonathan Brooks
THE BLACK MONK	Newton Pittman
VARVARA NIKOLAEVNA	Maryam Baig

Ensemble

NADIA	Stefanie Tovar
MIKHAIL	Ian Sinclair
YAKOV	Parker Hornsby
WORKERS, BELLMAN, HOTEL STAFF	Ryan Lescalleet, Parker Hornsby, Ian Sinclair

Musicians

PIANIST	Ariana Cook
VIOLINIST	Reynaldo Patiño

The Undermain Theatre (Katherine Owens, Artistic Director; Bruce DuBose, Executive Producer; Suzanne Thomas, Associate Producer) in Dallas, Texas, on April 4, 2009. Directed by Katherine Owens; scenic design by John Arnone; costume design by Bryan Wofford; lighting design by Steve Woods; scenic artists, Linda Noland and Robert Winn; music and sound design by Bruce DuBose; assistant scenic designer, Jeffrey Franks; assistant director, Lily Janiak; stage manager, Stew Awalt.

CAST

Principals (in order of appearance)

YEGOR SEMYONITCH PESOTSKY—renowned horticulturist, in his sixties, owner of a flourishing estate.

TANYA—Pesotsky's daughter, a childhood friend to Kovrin. She's in her twenties.

ORLOV—a valet—elderly, earnest, and put-upon.

ANDREI VASILICH KOVRIN—scholar and idealist in his thirties, an orphan raised by Pesotsky.

THE BLACK MONK—a visitor, a trickster, a friend.

VARVARA NIKOLAEVNA—strong and bolstering, in her forties or fifties.

Ensemble

NADIA—in her twenties, a friend to Tanya, has a beautiful singing voice.

MIKHAIL—in his thirties, he is Nadia's companion and a friend to Tanya and Pesotsky; he plays the piano.

YAKOV—in his twenties, a friend to Nadia and Mikhail, he would like to court Tanya.

The following can be doubled using actors playing Nadia, Mikhail, and Yakov, and one or two others:

CONCIERGE

BELLMAN

PEASANTS

ACT ONE

SCENE ONE

*Borissovka: the orchard on the estate of YEGOR SEMYO-
NITCH PESOTSKY. Smoke rises from the ground. Peasants tend the fires, heads bowed. Pesotsky, bundled against
the cold, stands raising a thermometer attached to the end
of a fourteen-foot pole. He raises it high and then lowers
and examines it.*

PESOTSKY
Terrible, terrible.
> *His daughter, TANYA, and SERVANT ORLOV arrive,
> both bundled up, and Pesotsky looks to them.*
No, no, it's coming. The star-filled sky declares it, and look how
the thermometer confirms it. Frost will come toward morning.
> *To Orlov, the servant.*
Where is Ivan Karlitch? Why isn't he here? Bring him here.

ORLOV
But he's gone. They say he went to town.

PESOTSKY
Who says? No, no, no. Find him, I say, now!

TANYA
I saw him drive off, Father. He's gone.

PESOTSKY
What kind of gardener is so idiotic that he leaves at such a
moment?
> *He whirls to Orlov.*
Find that miserable fool, I tell you, Orlov, and bring him here!

ORLOV
I will, I will, but I don't know where he is.

ANDREI VASILICH KOVRIN enters, carrying his suitcase.

KOVRIN
Hello. Hello.

TANYA
Father. It's Kovrin!

PESOTSKY
Has he come?
Hastening to Kovrin.
There he is! Kovrin!
But after a mere pat, he races on.
Forgive us, but your arrival brings you into the middle of our great anxiety.

KOVRIN
Yegor Semyonitch, whatever your mood, I am overjoyed to see you. What's the trouble?

PESOTSKY
Our bitter enemy is upon us.

TANYA
It's the frost, we're afraid of the frost, and Father says it must come by morning.

PESOTSKY
There is no doubt. And our wretched gardener has abandoned us.
Nearby, a peasant has fallen to his side in sleep, and Pesotsky pokes him with the stick to wake him.
But what else should I expect from these shiftless creatures who care only for vodka and the quickest road away from their duty.

KOVRIN
Tanya, take my hand.

He reaches out and she moves to greet him, but Pesotsky
sweeps her away.

PESOTSKY
The hour is most inopportune, Kovrin! The fires must not go out,
and so we haven't a second to attend you fully.

KOVRIN
Ignore me in every way. I don't care. I am glad to be here, whatever
the crisis.

PESOTSKY
Let me hug you. Let me hug you.
Hurrying back to hug Kovrin.
What a fine young man you are!
Studying him.
Kovrin, Kovrin, you have come. What joy I feel. But not now.
Tomorrow the sun will shine. But tonight we must take up the
struggle.
Moving off.
It's sad, but the second we turn our backs, the fires will go out.
He spies another peasant fallen to his side and so must
rouse him.
These lugs who eat my bread in the name of work they never do
would rather sleep than save my trees.
Advancing on another drowsy peasant.
Never mind that damage from the frost could cost me thousands
in good money, and then who would buy their bread for them?
The peasant rouses himself as Pesotsky nears.
Not that money can measure the value of the orchard. There's no
fortune in the world, no matter how vast, that could make up for
the loss of one little tree!

KOVRIN
What can I do? Assign me a task. I want to help.

      TANYA
But you must be ready to drop, Kovrin. You've been traveling for days.

      KOVRIN
I should be tired, I suppose. But I'm not!

      PESOTSKY
Good Lord, she's right. Be honest—you must be hungry and worn out after your journey. Forgive our rudeness, but we are embattled.
      Addressing Tanya.
I'll take first shift, Tanya, and you see Kovrin to his room.

      KOVRIN
Actually, I'm not ready for bed.

      TANYA
I'm very much awake, too, Father. I don't think I could sleep at all right now.

      PESOTSKY
No, no, no, Tanya, you look like you haven't slept in days.

      TANYA
You're the one who looks a wreck, Father. Tell him, Kovrin.

      PESOTSKY
Is she right?

      KOVRIN
Well, I must—

      PESOTSKY
Oh, don't say it. I surrender. I'm too tired to argue. But I'll come to you at three o'clock, Tanya.
      He hands her the thermometer on the stick.

And then you can sleep in the morning as long as you want.
Picking up the suitcase, and starting off.
Kovrin, come along. If I can't be the perfect host, at least I can brew some tea and show you to your room.

KOVRIN

Yegor Semyonitch, I guess I didn't make my point. Just to be here—to see you both—I feel somewhat ardent. Even wild. I want to stay with Tanya.

PESOTSKY

But . . . you're our guest.

KOVRIN

I'm asking. You know you're going to go to sleep and that will leave me all by myself, when all I want is to be with at least one of you now that I am here.

PESOTSKY

Do you know, I think I said it, but if I didn't, I will say it now—I'm too tired to argue. Anyway, it's a fine idea. You will keep her company. But take my coat. It's cold and getting colder.
Removing his coat, he helps Kovrin put it on.
Look at you. Let me give you one more hug before I go.
And he does.
There, there. Yes it's you, Kovrin. Goodnight.
Grabbing the suitcase, moving off.

KOVRIN

Goodnight.

PESOTSKY

Yes, yes. Goodnight to the two of you. Protect my wonderful trees. They sprout from my soul, you know.

TANYA

Goodnight, Father.

Watching, as Kovrin looks after Pesotsky.
Welcome to Borissovka. You come for vacation and are put to
work without sleep.

KOVRIN
I think it must be said, Tanya, that I volunteered.

TANYA
We both did. Let's walk. As father said, I must march about as a
kind of sentry.
She moves off, and he joins her.

KOVRIN
Well, good. I'm ready for anything. But what is it we're doing
again?

TANYA
Protecting the orchard from the frost.

KOVRIN
By walking about among these trees in their regimented rows?

TANYA
Kovrin, it's the fires. We need the smoke.

KOVRIN
Well, of course. We must have black thick smoke.

TANYA
Not us. The trees. Kovrin, certainly you remember that cloudy
weather protects the trees, because of how it keeps away the morning frost, and so when the sky is clear, we must provide the clouds.

KOVRIN
Was this true when I was a child?

TANYA
Yes, Kovrin. It's a fact, but apparently one you and your fancy friends at the university have no interest in.

KOVRIN
Halting as she walks on.
I think I need a moment. Have I come to the wrong estate? Who are you?

TANYA
Oh, stop it.

KOVRIN
No, no, I must find out. Such a serious face, a little pale with the cold. Such fine dark eyebrows. Wait, wait—let me look. Good heavens. It's Tanya Pesotsky, and she's all grown up.

TANYA
You've been gone eight years, you know.

KOVRIN
Seven.

TANYA
Eight, Kovrin.

KOVRIN
Whatever it is—in my mind I see you as I last saw you. Scrawny, long-legged, your hair flopping around your shoulders, so that—

TANYA
I know! So that I looked like a heron.

KOVRIN
Yes, a skinny, long-legged heron!

TANYA
Are you going to start it up again?

KOVRIN
But it is what you looked like.

TANYA
And now?

KOVRIN
No. No more.

TANYA
It bursts out of her.
Are we still your kindred people, Andryusha? I have to know.

KOVRIN
What?

TANYA
You're off with your wonderful, fascinating life away in Moscow at the university! But please tell me you don't feel you've outgrown us. I want so much to have you still think of us as your family.

KOVRIN
Of course I do.

TANYA
Be honest.

KOVRIN
Tanya, the way your father and you took me in when I had no one, after my mother . . . I have no other family.

TANYA
Because Father considers you his son—I know it—not his blood

son, of course, but somehow his own. I have to warn you not to be too surprised when you see all the photographs. Just be prepared.

KOVRIN
What photographs?

TANYA
Spotting a nearby sleeping peasant.
Look at that sleeping donkey.
She moves to the peasant, pokes him.
You! You! Wake up and stay awake. You cannot let the fires go out!

PEASANT ONE
I'm sorry.

TANYA
Just do your duty.
To Kovrin.
Now you see why we must be out here.

KOVRIN
Tanya. I think I have to know. What photographs?

TANYA
They're all over the house and all of you. Photographs of you, Kovrin. They're as plentiful as the leaves on the trees.

KOVRIN
I don't understand.

TANYA
I don't either, except I think my father loves you more than anyone else in the world. Because you are brilliant, you are accomplished. And since he raised and educated you, I think he believes your success is at least partly due to his influence.
She spies a sleeping peasant.

Oh, now look. Another sleeping fool.
> *Rushing over.*

Little Dunce, what are you doing? Let me help you.
> *Turning to Kovrin.*

They are like children. Or clumsy puppies. This is my life, Kovrin. Thank God you've come.

KOVRIN

Tanya. I must tell you. It's so amazing. I was with a doctor friend, who was advising me that in his opinion the thing I needed most was a chance to get away, to spend time in the country. No sooner had I returned to my apartment than I found your letter inviting me to come here for a visit.

TANYA

On that very day, Kovrin?

KOVRIN

Yes!

TANYA

Because I was thinking about you constantly. Even in dreams. I had to write that letter, I had to send it.

KOVRIN
> *He sings very softly, shyly.*

"Onyegin, Onyegin, I won't conceal it; I madly, madly love Tatiana . . ." I feel blessed to be here and to see you in this place with its smoke and stink and lazy peasants. I cherish it all. Every little—

PESOTSKY
> *Calling from offstage.*

Tanya! Kovrin!
> *Pesotsky enters far from them.*

TANYA
Father, we're over here!

PESOTSKY
I don't see you.

TANYA
Waving.
Here! Here!

PESOTSKY
Ah, yes, I have found you. You've done your work well, Tanya.
You may sleep at last.

TANYA
He's very good company, Father. The hours flew by.

PESOTSKY
Good, good. Still, you need your sleep.
Retrieving the thermometer on the stick.
And you, Kovrin, it's a wonder you can keep your eyes open.

KOVRIN
Actually, Yegor Semyonitch, I'm wide awake.

PESOTSKY
You can't mean it. How can that be?

KOVRIN
I don't know. But it's true. I'll stay with you now.

TANYA
I'm tempted to stay up, too, but I know I'll fall apart tomorrow if
I don't get some sleep.
As she heads off.
Goodnight to you both.

12.

PESOTSKY
Goodnight, my perfect daughter.
Tanya waves as she goes.

KOVRIN
Yes, my little heron-no-more, goodnight to you.
Kovrin watches her go, then looks back to see Pesotsky raising the thermometer to the farthest inch possible.

PESOTSKY
So this is the sad story, Kovrin. The surface of the ground is covered in frost; but stick a thermometer fourteen feet up into the air and it's warm. Look.
As he lowers the thermometer to show to Kovrin.
Do you see?

KOVRIN
Why does that happen?

PESOTSKY
I must say that, with all your education, I'd hoped you might tell me. But then, a man can't know everything. The biggest brain can't find a box in it for every fact. So what is your brain full of these days, in the sense of—what is your main interest at the university?

KOVRIN
Well, Yegor Semyonitch, philosophy, of course.

PESOTSKY
Philosophy still?

KOVRIN
Yes. I do some psychology, but mainly it's—

PESOTSKY
And it does not bore you?

KOVRIN
Bore me? No. I love it.

PESOTSKY
Well, then you're a lucky man. An unusual man, and lucky.

KOVRIN
It's difficult, however, you must understand. I have adversaries who condemn my principles. Entrenched scholars who oppose me and say I am too original—why can't I adopt the established methods? It wears me out.
> *Two sleepy peasants, heads down, are dragging a large bale of dung straw. Each has a rope over his shoulder attached to the straw as they trudge wearily along behind Pesotsky and Kovrin.*

PESOTSKY
You must stand up for yourself.

KOVRIN
I know.

PESOTSKY
No easy thing in philosophy. It's all in the air. Where is it?

KOVRIN
But that's its joy. Its greatness, because it's in the unknown—the eternal, and—
> *As Pestosky sees the dung straw being dragged by, the two men collide with a tree, one man going to the right of the tree, the other going to the left so that the bale bumps into the tree.*

PESOTSKY
My God! MY GOD, NOO! NOO!

KOVRIN
What is it? What?

PESOTSKY
God forgive us all! THESE WRETCHED SCOUNDRELS ARE
TANGLED IN MY TREE!
Racing toward them.
You're devils, a plague! They have spoiled it completely; nothing is
left but filth and devastation. The orchard is ruined, the orchard is
lost. My God, I—I—
At the cowering workers.
YOU ACCURSED FOOLS, WHAT AM I TO DO?

WORKER
Master, we were dragging the dung straw for the fires and—

PESOTSKY
Kovrin, listen to him! What's he saying? I don't understand him!
What am I to do with these hopeless people? He tells me he's drag-
ging dung straw—yes, I know that, I see that. But he does not say
why he must collide with the tree. Why do they not walk on the
same side? Nothing more is required! WALK ON THE SAME
SIDE OF THE TREE! Drag the dung, BUT AVOID THE
TREE!
Touching the tree tenderly.
Look how their ropes lashed into it. These wounds in the bark. Do
you see them?

WORKERS ONE & TWO
Forgive us, sir!
Please.
Having untangled the ropes, the workers are going.

PESOTSKY
Calling after them.
Hanging is too good for both of you!
And to Kovrin.

I can't beat them. I want to, but I am too kindhearted. They take advantage of me. Anyway, what am I to do?

Weary, looking for a place to rest.

I'm thirsty, and still half asleep. The little sleep I managed was all broken up, and . . .

But looking at Kovrin, he is full of feeling.

God bless you, God bless you! I'm very glad you are here.

Moving to Kovrin, embracing him.

But it's more than glad. I don't have the words. I am indescribably glad. Thank you.

Looking up.

Ah! The sun. Morning, morning. Look how the garden welcomes the light.

Gazing at the sunlight he loves.

In the night the clear sky is a villain, but in daylight, well, it's a wonder.

Starting to go.

Come, let me show you my new greenhouses, there's three of them, and the covered garden. . . . Every visitor who beholds them calls them "the marvel of the century."

He stops, seeing that Kovrin hasn't moved but stands looking up into the light.

What's wrong? Is something wrong?

KOVRIN

No, no, it just struck me. Once I was a little boy running and playing in this orchard. I was happy here.

PESOTSKY

You've come for the whole summer.

Returning to him.

What am I doing? We can see the greenhouses and all that later.

Moving toward the house.

Come. We'll have some tea.

KOVRIN

I remember wonderful antique porcelain teacups. Do you still have
them?

PESOTSKY

Without a doubt.

KOVRIN

I would like tea in them. Tea with cream and rich shortbreads.

PESOTSKY

We'll have it all. Tea and cups and cream and shortbreads. Yes,
yes.

*Pesotsky goes, and Kovrin, lagging behind, turns to the au-
dience, speaking to them.*

KOVRIN

Isn't it this way always? Always and for everyone forever. We go
home and it happens. Some slight detail transports us.

*As music starts—a piano—Kovrin moves downstage to a
small extension that juts out from the front edge of the
stage. It is a miniature thrust that seems to separate
him from the world. He continues to the audience, as
to a friend.*

Trifles arise and fill us, overtaking us with our childhood.

Pesotsky steps back out.

PESOTSKY

Kovrin, what are you doing? Come along.

KOVRIN

Yes, yes, Yegor Semyonitch. I'll be there.

To the audience once more.

Tomorrow I know what I'll do. Walking quickly off that way will
bring us to the river.

Pointing off.

A steep clay bank. Pine trees tower. Sandpipers fret along the shore. Gazing into those dark waters, one is overtaken by the desire to sit down and write a ballad.

Once more, Pesotsky is seen, calling.

PESOTSKY
Kovrin, Kovrin, you silly boy, come! I demand it.

KOVRIN
Yes, yes!
To the audience.
My vacation has begun.
He turns and hurries off.
As the music continues, with perhaps singing added in.

SCENE TWO

The music continues, bridging with the change of light into the Pesotsky home. There are chairs, a couch, and Tanya is found near the piano with visiting neighbors, MIKHAIL, NADIA, and YAKOV. One plays the piano, another the violin. Nadia sings beautifully. Pesotsky is seated on the couch facing out and happily listening, as the song comes to an end.

PESOTSKY
Wonderful, wonderful, my angels. What's next?

MIKHAIL
Let's play the Schubert.

NADIA
No, not that.

YAKOV
What do you want?

NADIA
The Serenade by Braga.

TANYA
I'm not in the mood.

NADIA
Well, I am.

PESOTSKY
It's lovely. Please do it. Where's Kovrin? Where is that boy? Tanya, make him come join us.

TANYA
I tried. But he was looking for something and he couldn't be bothered.

PESOTSKY
He adores the music.

TANYA
I know, but he'd lost a very important book. It was very important.

PESOTSKY
Books. The boy is a bedlam of books. And work.
Several books lie on the couch and he picks one up.
But then they are his work, these books. And he never sleeps. I go to bed at night and he's awake.
Rising with the book, pacing to the guests, entertaining them.
I rise with the chickens and there he is, so I start to think that he never sleeps. Except that, upon occasion on this very couch—
Returning to the couch.
—where I am sitting now—where I am about to sit. Tilting into sitting. It is the wine that makes me tilt, along with the axe of the years cutting away at my knees.

But he manages to sit.

But I was saying something else. My subject was a splendid matter. Far better than this discourse on age and knees and tilting, but I have no idea what it was.

  As Kovrin walks into the room carrying a book, a manuscript.

Oh, yes! It was Kovrin! And the way I find him sleeping right here on this couch. By accident in the afternoon. I've seen him. And the dire consequences of such a nap is that he stays awake all night. Sleepless until morning.

  Back up on his feet, he approaches Kovrin.

And then he finds himself wide awake and cheerful, as if it's all just the way he wants it. It's a great mistake on God's part, I say, to waste such energy on a scholar. Drink some wine. I wanted your company.

KOVRIN
Now you have it. I'd like a cigar.

PESOTSKY
That's right. You work too hard. The girls want you out here. They need some charm to distract them from the wearisome noise I've been making, which they politely—

KOVRIN
Listen to him!
  To everyone.
One of the most distinguished men in all of Russia and he's begging for a compliment!

PESOTSKY
I am a doddering composition, and these beautiful young girls are bored with me.

KOVRIN
I think they hang on your every word. Nadia. Sit next to Yegor.
  Laughing a little, Nadia hurries to Pesotsky.

And smile and ask him to tell you about his hothouses and his covered garden and—

PESOTSKY

No, no, no. Don't start making mischief.
To Nadia, beside him.
But I will tell you one thing I am completely correct about and there can be no argument.
To Kovrin.
You work too hard!
Back to Nadia.
He works without rest.

KOVRIN

With wine and cigar.
I must admit there's no restraining me. I've come to the country to rest, but I'm as passionately immersed in my work as I was at the university. Even more so. I read and read, I make a note, and then I read some more. There are not enough hours in the day—and when I have a spare minute, I use it to study Italian.

NADIA

Buon giorno, dove stai?

KOVRIN

Caro mio ben.

NADIA

Mangi e beri tutti i giorni.

KOVRIN

Si. Vuol balare senor contigo.
Everyone is very entertained by this, as if by a party trick.

PESOTSKY

Look at that. Soon they'll be able to converse in that delightful language.

*Nadia stays close to Kovrin, following him as Tanya
watches.*

It's as if I'm happy here, Yegor Semyonitch. And it's all so simple.
Each morning I have coffee. I chat with Tanya, as she drinks her
tea, and we talk. Little things. This and that. Nothing really. Then
I go for a long walk, and I know that soon I'll be at my desk. My
powers of concentration have become the strongest they've ever
been in my life. I take good clear notes. I read. I think. And there
are moments when I stop. Everything. I sit and I look out the
window, and this may sound unusual, it is strange—but my body
fills with delight. I feel as if I might evaporate.

PESOTSKY

Well, let's hope you don't, my boy.

KOVRIN

I think it comes from this present time which is so satisfying, and
somehow it's all merging with sensations reawakened from my
childhood here, and in this mood I start back to work. Soon I will
have something to show those fools at the university that will make
their heads explode. They think they can judge me. I hate them
with every drop of blood in my veins.
Suddenly to Tanya.
Tanya, there was a part of the garden that was utterly fantastic. It
was a kind of playground. Do you know what I'm talking about?

TANYA

Yes, of course. But I think, Nadia, we should get back to the music.
She takes Nadia by the arm, and the girls head to the piano.

KOVRIN

There were trees cut in these fanciful, fantastic shapes. You must
remember.

TANYA

Of course.

KOVRIN

But where is it?

> *As the girls seem interested only in the music, he turns to Pesotsky on the nearby couch.*

I had forgotten about it, until just the other day. And when I went to look for it, it was nowhere to be found. Yegor Semyonitch, it was so beautiful, what happened to it?

PESOTSKY

I did away with it. I came to see it as folly, a kind of mockery of my real aims, and so I had it destroyed.

KOVRIN

> *Joining Pesotsky on the couch.*

I remember apple trees bent and bound into the shapes of archways. Blooming branches were cut into crests and star shapes. I adored it.

PESOTSKY

Well, I destroyed it.

KOVRIN

It was a wonderland.

PESOTSKY

Say what you want, Kovrin, my view of the facts remains unaltered!

> *More or less joking.*

It was folly, and you work too hard!

> *The musicians start up, playing the violin and piano, while Nadia sings Braga's* Serenade. *Kovrin and Pesotsky sit facing out as they listen. After a measure or two, Kovrin looks to Pesotsky.*

KOVRIN

Excuse me, but—

PESOTSKY
Shhhhhhh. Listen.
> *They listen a little more.*

KOVRIN
> *Hushed.*
Yes, yes, but I don't quite get it. What is it?

PESOTSKY
> *Hushed.*
What?

KOVRIN
> *Hushed.*
The music, the lyrics, what do they—I don't understand.
> *They listen a little more.*

PESOTSKY
> *Hushed.*
Surely, it's obvious.
> *Kovrin listens, trying.*

KOVRIN
No.
> *Another interlude as they listen.*

PESOTSKY
Surely, you see. It's nothing more than this young girl, this maiden
who's more or less ill with magical desires.
> *Nodding to Kovrin.*

KOVRIN
Oh. Yes.

PESOTSKY
You see what I'm getting at.
> *Kovrin nods, and Pesotsky returns his attention to Nadia*

and the song. He listens, then speaks, his attention split, so he speaks intermittently, a kind of counterpoint to her voice.

And then one night from her garden comes some sort of music. . . . Very unusual music . . . gratifying but with a nature that bewilders her, leaves her guessing . . . and then, after some time passes, she begins to see the fact of the matter, which is more or less . . . that the music is a sacred harmony, which mortals, of which she is one . . . can never understand, and which, therefore, must leave her . . . alone . . . and go flying back up to heaven.

Nadia sings another bar or two, and Pesotsky listens dreamily until the song ends. He loves the song, her voice, and as the singing ends, he glances at Kovrin and finds that Kovrin has fallen asleep beside him on the couch.

Goodness. Look at that.

Hushed, but enlisting the other guests.

I tell him something and he falls asleep. What a landmark! I talk of it and it occurs, just as I described it. He's sleeping on the couch!

Everyone looks as Tanya glides up behind Kovrin, leans close and whispers to him.

TANYA
Kovrin, Kovrin, did we sing you a lullaby?
He stirs, looks about.

KOVRIN
Oh, no. Good Lord.
As everyone laughs warmly, he gets to his feet, startled, looking about.
Look at me. I'm going for a walk. I'm embarrassed. Then I'll be fine.

TANYA
I'll come with you.
He heads off, and Tanya hurries after him.

PESOTSKY
Calling after him.
Let's hope you sleep tonight.

TANYA
Calling back.
It's our fault, Father!
They move off together, down and away from the couch and the others who, all except Pesotsky, retreat and gather around the piano, where they hum to the music in lowering light. Pesotsky remains on the couch, lingering in the spell of the music as the light goes dim on him. Colorful leaves, as if blown by a wind, fall from above over Tanya and Kovrin.
We should have sung something more lively and enthusiastic.

KOVRIN
No, no. It wasn't the music.

TANYA
The truth is, Kovrin, I find that serenade almost hypnotic.

KOVRIN
No, no. It's something else entirely. I've been thinking all day of it, and growing more and more frustrated. It's this book—the one I was looking for. It contains a legend that I—

TANYA
What legend?

KOVRIN
I can't stop thinking about it.

TANYA
Is it famous?

KOVRIN

I'm fascinated by it and I feel the need to . . . but I can't find the book it's in. I've looked everywhere.

TANYA

Could I have heard of it?

KOVRIN

Of course you could have, but it's unlikely, because I have the feeling the source is esoteric. But it tells how one thousand years ago, a monk, dressed in black, walked into the desert in Arabia. He walked over the sand, up and down the dunes, and in those very same minutes, fishermen hundreds of miles away saw a black monk gliding over the surface of a lake.

At the piano, someone plays.

This second monk was a mirage. Now don't try to apply the laws of optics, because the legend pays no attention to them. Just listen to the rest. The mirage of the monk at the lake produced another identical mirage above it, and from that one came another, and on and on so that almost instantly, the image of The Black Monk was sent endlessly from one level of the atmosphere to the next, resulting in The Black Monk being seen in Africa and in Spain. There were Italians who saw him. People in the far north. And all at the same time. And then he sailed right out of the earth's atmosphere into the heavens.

This leaves him gazing up and out at the star-filled sky.

And there he has roamed ever since, never finding the right conditions that might allow him to fade away. At the moment he might be seen on Mars, or near a star in the Southern Cross.

Glancing at Tanya, who also gazes skyward.

But the main point, the heart of the whole legend, is that exactly one thousand years from the day that monk first stepped into the desert, the mirage will come back to the earth . . .

Once again he studies the heavens as if expecting to see The Black Monk.

. . . and people will see it. According to the legend, the thousand years is coming to an end. So we should be expecting The Black Monk any day now.

For a second, they scan the sky together.

TANYA
Wheeling away, playfully, as if to fend off The Black Monk.
So he's coming? Shall we all duck our heads and hide our eyes?

KOVRIN
I don't know what we should or shouldn't do, but—

TANYA
I'm teasing.

KOVRIN
Yes, well. And you're right to do it. It is what I need. I'll try to be amused.

TANYA
Seeing she has annoyed him, or even hurt his feelings.
I don't think I care much for this legend.

KOVRIN
Well, let's discard it, then. We'll drop it from all the various collections of world myths. Not that it matters, because the truly silly part is that I have no idea where on earth I first ran into it. I read so much, it shouldn't surprise me that I've lost track. But I feel that an understanding of this legend would assist me in my work. That it would ignite my work.
Stepping out from the area of the piano, Nadia calls.

NADIA
Tanya, come back, will you? We have to ask you something.

KOVRIN
You better go.

TANYA
To Kovrin.
Come with us.

KOVRIN
No, I want to walk a little and meditate on . . . I don't know what.
These flowers and their irritating odor.

TANYA
They've just been watered.

KOVRIN
Well, that explains it.

NADIA
Tanya, you're going to cause a problem!

TANYA
Moving toward Nadia, she calls to Kovrin.
I'll come back as soon as I can. You wait here.

NADIA
Waving as she and Tanya go.
Good-bye, Kovrin.

KOVRIN
Bye-bye.
*He looks to the audience and seems to need to defend him-
self.*
Well, it's true. These flower beds have a humid smell! There's an
aggression in them, a kind of assault. With a slight twist to the
normal sense of things one could say, "these flowers stink." This
smells good, that smells bad.
Ripping flowers up from the ground.
Well, these flowers stink!
Then he stares at them.
What's wrong with me? Look at them. They're in fact lovely.

Picking the petals, studying them.

Layer upon layer of delicate petals. To what end? To what end, Kovrin, this beauty?

At the piano indoors, music starts up again, singing, with the violin prominent.

Listen. What an instrument. Full of feeling—but unable to express itself precisely. And yet so . . . I should probably wait here as Tanya asked. Or go back and join them.

Looking around.

But why do that, when I can . . . follow that path to the river. Let's say I'm adrift. Without decision. Along the steep bank, among the bare roots. Down to the water.

He hurries down toward the audience, and as he does, there is the squawk of startled ducks.

Oh, I've startled them. Poor ducks!

Looking down as if into water, then up as if calling after the departing ducks.

I'm sorry, good friends, I mean no harm. But fly if you must into the last of the sun. Although you might beware those distant pines whose mood grows gloomy.

Now, somewhat puzzled, he looks down.

And on the surface of the river it's already night.

The violin plays again, and he listens.

In that violin, I hear the cry of a human soul.

Intimately, to the audience.

Do you know this feeling? A solitary dusk in which one feels that all the world might be understood at last. How open it is here. And the breeze.

The sound of the breeze.

Hear it? It's in my hair. It moves around me and on to bend the rye in the field and then further on, flowing until it enters in those distant pines, where—

Freezing, looking.

What is that?

Pointing, telling the audience.

There's something. Climbing.

Huge shadows fill the stage, a towering shape rising up behind him.

Black. Look! The outline isn't clear . . . but . . .

He turns and finds a gigantic shadow or silhouette of THE BLACK MONK.

. . . but there can be no doubt that it's speeding. Closer.

Now The Black Monk steps out of the shadows. He's a man of medium height, with black hair and eyebrows, a pale face, dressed in a dark hooded robe, barefoot, a seeming beggar. Kovrin looks in delight and amazement, and then he presents The Black Monk to the audience.

Look who it is. The thousand years must be over and he's here.

Closely watching The Black Monk, who studies him.

Does he see me? I think he sees me. I think he's looking at me.

And now The Black Monk turns to the audience.

Is he looking at you? Does he see you? I think he sees you.

He looks back and forth between audience and The Black Monk.

I would say—I would say—he sees us all! And he smiles. And nods. An affectionate smile I would say. Even tender. Don't you think? But sly. Yes, sly. But mainly gentle. And what a pale, thin face, so—

But now The Black Monk begins to move.

Oh! Now what? He's—going!? Is this the end? Without a word. Without—

The Black Monk keeps going.

Yes, yes, he's off! On his way away!

Kovrin watches as The Black Monk joins with the gigantic shadow, which moves off.

He grows large again. Vast and strange, he flies over the river toward the mountains!

As if watching The Black Monk fly off, he turns out, moves to the miniature thrust.

He doesn't seem to see them! He's going to crash into the rocks!

Worried but not loud.

Please, no. Look out.

He turns to the audience.

But, no. Without a sound, he entered into those stony bluffs, disappearing like wind.

He tries to fathom it all.

Well, there you see. That means the legend's true. He was here and we saw him. Not only his black monk's clothes, but his eyes and smile, his—

Tanya, in the area of the piano, calls to him, then starts toward him.

TANYA

Kovrin, Kovrin! What are you doing? Come up here!

KOVRIN

What? What? Did something happen?

TANYA

Arriving.

Well, you ran away! I told you to wait and you ran away. That's what happened!

KOVRIN

No, no. Something else! Did you see him?

TANYA

Who?

KOVRIN

I'm sorry. What?

TANYA

Oh just come up! Don't you want our company?

KOVRIN

Whirling to the audience.

I thought she might have seen him, but . . . I should have known. Their music continued without the slightest interruption. Or did it? I don't really know.

To a particular audience member.
Do you remember?

TANYA
Kovrin. I want to dance. Will you dance with me? Everyone's dancing and . . . I would so like—

KOVRIN
I can't! Please forgive me, but I can't.
Back to the audience.
I want to tell her, but what will she think? It will only frighten her.

TANYA
I should have known you wouldn't. Everyone said you wouldn't.

KOVRIN
To the audience.
I must find the book.
As he wheels upstage.
I must find that book.
Kovrin hurries up to a chair where some of his books are in a suitcase, and there he starts searching through them. At the same time, Tanya rejoins the party near the piano, and the party continues in half light with people dancing, the music faint. Also at the same time, lights come up on Pesotsky still sitting on the couch, eyeing Kovrin as he searches.

PESOTSKY
Look at how things are! Is anything what it seems?
Kovrin takes note of Pesotsky.
I ask you. I don't think so! But still, I ask you!
He crosses to Kovrin, who continues to examine one book after another.
Here I am—they give me medals. "Pesotsky," they say, "grows apples the size of a man's head," and "Pesotsky," they say, "has made a fortune with his orchard." As far as they're concerned, it's

all wonderful. The orchard is famous and bountiful. I'm famous and everything is wonderful. But there is a question, and the question is: what is it all for? Today my orchard is not merely a wonder but an institution, because it embodies a step forward into the new era of our industry and economy.

Turning, he wanders back toward the couch.

But what, I must ask, is it for? What is the purpose? Kovrin, I ask you: what is the purpose?

KOVRIN

Yegor Semyonitch, are you really asking me?

PESOTSKY

I am. Yes.

KOVRIN

But you more than anyone else must know.

Rising, carrying a book, he walks toward Pesotsky.

PESOTSKY

Yes, yes, I must. But I don't. You see, that's what I'm saying. I'm asking. I have no idea.

KOVRIN

Joining Pesotsky on the couch.

Well, a business whose nature is to grow things, to have beauty and abundance everywhere, must produce its own reward.

PESOTSKY

No, no. I don't mean like that. I mean to ask: what will happen to the orchard when I die?

He plucks the book from Kovrin's hands.

As you see it now, it wouldn't last a month without me. It is a success; it is a gigantic success, but the whole secret is not how much fruit the orchard gives us, and it's not the many workers we employ, but the secret to the success is that I love it. Do you understand? I love the dirt. I love the work. Perhaps more than I love myself. Look at me: I do everything. I work from morning till night. All the grafting—I do myself. All the pruning. The planting. Everything. I do it myself! If someone dares assist me, I get suspicious and jealous, because they can't possibly care as much as I do. Because the whole secret lies in the devoted eye of the master, the loving touch of his hands. It's the feeling when I go to visit somewhere and I sit there unable to relax, because my heart is restless, I am not myself, because I am worrying, I am afraid that something bad is happening in the garden! That's how I live. And who's going to look after it all when I die? The workers? The gardener? No. Never. Because the true enemy of our business isn't the may bug; it isn't the hungry rabbit, or the frost in the cloudless morning. It's the one who doesn't care! It's the one who loves only the money. The entrepreneur!

> *Behind them, the party has ended as they've talked, the guests leaving one by one, until Tanya is alone; she glides up and kisses her father goodnight on the cheek.*

TANYA
Goodnight.

> *As Tanya leaves, Kovrin follows her with his gaze, then turns to Pesotsky.*

KOVRIN
But Yegor Semyonitch, Tanya will be here. Tanya would always protect the garden, you know that.

PESOTSKY
Of course. If I died and everything belonged to Tanya, and she were to run it all with devotion, well, thank God.

> *But then he whispers, as if suggesting a crime.*

But what about this? What if she gets married? And then she has children. God forbid, but I must say it, because then she would have no time for the garden. It frightens me; and what frightens me most of all is that she could end up marrying some greedy fool who will rent out my orchard to merchants, who will run it not with love but only to get rich. If one of those who loves only money ever got his hands on this beautiful place, everything would go to ruin before I was dead and buried one little year! In our business, women are the scourge of God!

KOVRIN
Yegor Semyonitch, you don't mean that.
Pesotsky rises and walks about in excitement.

PESOTSKY
No, no, just listen to me. Don't concern yourself with what I'm saying. Just listen. Perhaps I'm selfish. It may be a matter of nothing more than my ego. All right, that's what it is. Still I will say it. I don't want Tanya to marry. I'm afraid of it. You saw that young fool before, that Yakov—he wears a monocle and a bow tie to impress her. He's an idiot, and Tanya will never marry him. I know she won't, but I can't stand seeing him. I can't stand it. I'm very odd, my boy, there's nothing to be done about it. I admit it; I am eccentric, there's no getting away from it. I've been out in the rain too many times and I've got rust in some important places, but—
He grimaces in sudden pain.
—but—Ohhh, ohhh.
Sort of doubling over and then half straightening, he rocks from one foot to the other.

KOVRIN
What is it, Yegor Semyonitch? What are you doing? Are you in pain?

PESOTSKY
No, no, it's nothing.
But still he rocks from one foot to the other, half doubled up.

KOVRIN
You look like you're in pain. Is it your stomach?

PESOTSKY

No. I'm trying to say something, and yet I can't. I can't bring myself to say it.

KOVRIN

But if it's so important, you must.

PESOTSKY

All right. I will throw open the window and let it out. I love you and I'm going to speak openly. In my dealings I have the reputation of facing head-on even the most ticklish questions. I say what I think. If I think it, I say it. In other words, I cannot stand so-called innermost thoughts. No, no, let them come out. And so I will tell you directly: you are the only man I would trust to give my daughter to in marriage. You are intelligent; you have a good heart; you would not allow my beloved business to come to ruin. But the main reason is—I love you like a son, and I'm proud of you. If some sort of romance were to start up between you and Tanya, I would be so happy. So happy.

> *They stand facing each other for several beats until Kovrin, baffled and a little embarrassed, laughs. Pesotsky laughs with him.*

Yes, yes, I suppose it's a joke. I can see that it's comical. Still, I say it.

> *Looking around, awkward, a little embarrassed himself, he hands Kovrin's book back to him.*

I think I'm keeping you from your books. Goodnight, my friend.

> *Moving to go.*

KOVRIN

Well, goodnight, Yegor Semyonitch.

PESOTSKY

Hesitating.

If you and Tanya had a son, I would make him a horticulturist. But these are silly dreams. Goodnight.

> *Pesotsky goes, leaving Kovrin, who turns to the audience in amazement.*

KOVRIN

The orchard. Of course he's worried about the orchard. He loves the orchard; it's his work, and—

He stops, steps toward them.

Marry Tanya? Did he mean it? The way he suffered about who would inherit his farm; the way he struggled to know its fate. You'd think he was in a war. Even here on this idyllic site. So is it that way for all men today? We must all be ready to defend ourselves, always prepared for battle. At the university, they say to me, "Is that your idea? That! You would like us to consider that!?" And they are openly disgusted.

Even more directly to the audience.

Do you have an idea? What is your idea? We have ideas. What else is in our heads? And so I must answer them, "Yes. It's mine. It's what I have. It is my thought." And if they're right? And it is disgusting. Is it not still mine?

Freezing, annoyed with himself.

No, no—no more thinking about orchards.

Grabbing and ringing a servant bell.

I need to work. I need to find that book in which the legend is described, so that I can more fully—

Again, he freezes and moves to the audience.

Marry Tanya? Did he mean it? Did he actually mean it?

Once more annoyed.

What am I doing thinking about such things? After what happened in that field. After what I saw. No, that is what matters. That is . . . Perhaps if I just close my eyes and think, the name of the book will come back to me.

Closing his eyes, standing very still.

If I close my eyes and think about the legend, about The Black Monk.

After a beat, his eyes still closed.

Do you know what? Thinking like this seems to dismiss all need to find the book. It's as if my questions have been answered even when they haven't. Yes. Thinking about The Black Monk suggests that thinking about The Black Monk is all I need to do. . . .

And then he's jolted, an electric current moving through him.

Oh, oh, what's this, what is this? Oh, oh!

>*The feeling courses through him and he sways with it.*

What is it? Stop, stop. Ohhhh!

>*He writhes with a deep and excessive pleasure that takes*
>*him down to the floor on his knees in a kind of bow, as*
>*Orlov enters and walks up from behind Kovrin, who does not*
>*see him.*

Everywhere inside me—in my blood—everywhere, I am touched, I am held, I am caressed.

ORLOV

Yes, sir.

KOVRIN

>*Looking up but having difficulty understanding.*

Orlov . . . ?

ORLOV

I heard the bell, sir.

KOVRIN

Yes, yes. Bring me wine. A bottle of Lafitte. As fast as you can!

ORLOV

Yes, sir.

>*Orlov goes.*

KOVRIN

I want to write.

>*Overtaken by a wild enthusiasm, leaping up, grabbing his*
>*notebook.*

I want to write. But what? What words? Let me begin with— No, no, not that—it's derivative. I want to come up with something powerful and new that people need. It must be needed by the world. I want to begin with our lives.

>*Orlov returns and stands waiting with a bottle of wine and a*
>*glass.*

The way we are what we are. And yet it must be unbounded. Utterly original and unbounded. Staggering.

At last seeing Orlov.

Oh, Orlov, yes, yes, you're here! Hello. Oh, my, that was quick. That was wonderful. The way you went away and now you're back. How are you? Sleepy, I would bet.

ORLOV

No.

KOVRIN

No? Not sleepy. How odd.

ORLOV

No, sir. Goodnight, sir.

Orlov goes, and Kovrin looks to the audience.

KOVRIN

All right. Good. I saw Orlov; he saw me; we saw one another. We spoke. I didn't scare him. He was fine.

Sipping wine, he lies back on the couch.

So it does no harm, this thing I'm in. The thousand years has come to an end, and there is no harm in it. No harm at all.

He lays there in the fading light. And then there is a loud crash from off, then a door slamming.

SCENE THREE

Lights up: shouts from offstage: daylight. Kovrin bolts up, tangled in his jacket, which is covering him as would a blanket. Another crash is followed by Tanya screaming, then Tanya stomps into the room.

TANYA

I can't stand it anymore. Oh, he's terrible, he's horrible. Why does he say these things to me?

KOVRIN
Who?

TANYA
I don't understand it!
Pesotsky enters and is surprised to find Kovrin there.

PESOTSKY
I'm not following her. I don't want to see her.

TANYA
Go away! Go away!
She tries to hide under the piano.

PESOTSKY
I don't want to talk to her. I'm not following her. This is my house, this is my room, my chairs, this is my sofa.

TANYA
And the air I need to breathe? Do you own that, too?

PESOTSKY
I'm just walking through my house. That's all I'm doing, you selfish little girl.

TANYA
Why are you trying to destroy my life?

PESOTSKY
No, no, I don't care about it. There are far more urgent matters crying out in the world on this morning.
On his way to the door.
I will not let you distract me. I have my duties. Responsibilities that I must—
Stopping, he looks at Kovrin.
No, no, I cannot keep it up. Her tears, her bitter words thrown at me, wound me. My own bitter words, thrown at her, wound me.

Returning to her.
Forgive me, little Tanya. I'm sorry.

TANYA
I don't care what you say!

PESOTSKY
Let's not fight. Please, I—

TANYA
Go away!
Hiding even further under the piano.

PESOTSKY
Kovrin, you see how impossible this is for me.

KOVRIN
What happened?

PESOTSKY
I don't know. It's just impossible.
Settling into a chair.
I'm depressed. I'm depressed.

TANYA
You do too know! You're cruel and belligerent and you must boss, boss, boss everybody in every possible way! I hate you. I hate you.

PESOTSKY
Tanya, I— Tanya, I—

TANYA
You will never hurt my feelings again!

PESOTSKY
Listen to me.

Moving a little toward her.
For just one minute and then—

TANYA

No! No, no! I don't want to hear it. I say, leave me alone!
Still he faces her, hoping.
You have to hear me, I'm screaming right at you. Leave me alone!

PESOTSKY

All right, then. Have it your way! I will never speak to you again for the remaining days of my life, as many or few as they may be. Nothing? Do you hear me? I swear it!

TANYA

Good. Good.

PESOTSKY

All right, then. Let it be good.
Once more he starts to leave.
We're both satisfied. Good-bye.
This time Pesotsky keeps going. When he is gone, Kovrin, still on the sofa tangled in his jacket, turns from him to Tanya, who remains on the floor under the piano.

KOVRIN

What is all this? And first thing in the morning. I need some coffee.
He rings a servant bell.

TANYA

If you knew how he humiliates me!

KOVRIN

You've had a fight, a disagreement, and—

TANYA

No. That's not it at all. I want to die. I made an innocent remark based on my love for the farm. All I did is suggest that we might do just as well with fewer full-time workers since we can always hire day-laborers.

Pacing about.

You must have noticed how the workers sit around doing nothing half the time. So for actually seeing a problem and actually making a suggestion, he screams at me. The first word out of his mouth is a curse, and then it's just insults and poison pouring out of him. What for? What did I do?

Running to him, she hurls herself sobbing into his arms on the couch.

I don't know. I don't know.

KOVRIN

There, there.

TANYA

He's ruined my life. Day after day he destroys my confidence, making me so confused and nervous I do nothing right when I'm around him. I try to show my talent for being a horticulturist, my love of the orchard, but I know he sees me as a liability. And so I say, all right, if I'm so inept, if I'm useless, I give up. I'll run away. I'll become a clerk for the telegraph company.

She burrows into his arms on the couch.

KOVRIN

Come, now, no, no. Where is Orlov? We must have some coffee. When people are angry, Tanya, everything gets exaggerated. I know he hurt your feelings, but you didn't exactly hold back with the things you—

Orlov steps in.

KOVRIN

There you are! Some coffee, please. And buns. Would you like some berries, Tanya?

TANYA
I'm not hungry.

KOVRIN
Bring her some strawberries and cream.
    As she trembles.
Look at you, your poor little shoulders are shaking, and your hands grab each other as if you have no one to care for you in the world. I'm the orphan, remember. You are in your father's house. Let me take your hand.
    He reaches, takes her hands.
It makes me sad to see you so upset when your trouble isn't really serious. Nothing has happened, yet you suffer as if some catastrophe has already struck.

TANYA
How can you say it's nothing when my father swears he will never speak to me again?

KOVRIN
He doesn't mean it. These are trifles. And maybe I can't stop them from ruining the morning. Perhaps they'll darken the whole day. But not another second more. I won't allow it.

TANYA
We're alone here too much—Father and me. We have only the orchard and after that the orchard. At night when I fall asleep, I dream of apples and bushes.
    As he smiles.
It's true. And our friends are boring. They're all boring. When you first went away to school and then you returned on holiday—I remember how the house grew bright, the windows, the furniture, you lifted some veil. And what if I'm like that—what if my true vocation is in some other realm, one utterly unknown to me, utterly unthought of, and yet I would be graceful and confident and clever there.

KOVRIN
Well, what could it be?

TANYA
I don't know. Because I'm here working for Father. Wherever I turn, it's his dream. Sometimes even my thoughts are things he's said or written. But your life is so different, you live in the city with your career and your freedom and you're only here for a visit, a little—

KOVRIN
Stopping her.
Tanya. It would be wrong of me to let you misunderstand my life. It isn't the perfect thing you imagine. But more importantly, the love that you and your father share is the spontaneous and un-judgmental love that flows only in the blood relations in a family. After my parents died, I believed I would go to my grave without ever knowing sincere affection again, and yet in this house I was blessed to touch it. Somehow the two of you were willing to share it. Your father loves you more than anything in the world.

TANYA
That's not what I'm talking about. And he doesn't.

KOVRIN
But he does. He loves you more than all the leaves and petals in all the orchards in the—

TANYA
Don't you hear anything I am saying!? Don't you care? I'm talk-ing to you—don't lecture me. You are yourself, and what you do, where you go, what you think is your own, it's all yours. And now you must sit there and tell me that I understand noth-ing, I am ungrateful. Yes, please explain Tanya Pesotsky to me, so that—!
She wheels, turning her back.
Oh, look what I'm doing! You try to tell me something honestly, but I must throw it out!

*She does not see Pesotsky, who has arrived to stand in the
doorway, bearing a tray with coffee and bread and berries,
but Kovrin, looking past her, sees him.*

What a terrible person I am, with such a hard little pebble of a
soul!

KOVRIN
Yegor Semyonitch.

PESOTSKY
It's true what you see. I am here. I contradict myself. I have the
coffee and strawberries and buns and black bread with salt. When
I came upon Orlov in the hallway, he seemed without a plan of
any kind. In fact he seemed to wander the halls as if they were a
wilderness and he had lost his compass. So I snatched the tray and
told him to go home and stay there. In fact, to go drown himself, if
he cared to.
        Moving to kneel before Tanya.
Tanya, my darling child, I beg you, I beg you, forgive me.

TANYA
No, no. It's you who must forgive me.

PESOTSKY
I see the truth now. I was wrong.

TANYA
The truth is I'm a fool who took the morning to demonstrate my
nature beyond all doubt.

PESOTSKY
No, no, you must not say such terrible things about yourself. A father's heart cannot stand it.

TANYA
You must forgive me.

PESOTSKY

Only if you forgive me.
As Pesotsky serves and she eats and drinks greedily.

TANYA

I do, I do, and I'm so hungry. And this coffee's wonderful.

PESOTSKY

Yes, well, fighting is hard work.

TANYA

With all my sobbing, I could have watered the orchards from end
to end.

KOVRIN
Standing up.
I think I'll go.

PESOTSKY

Kovrin, no.

TANYA

Please stay.

PESOTSKY

Kovrin, yes. I feel you have been our peacemaker.

KOVRIN

No, no, it is your hearts: your love that makes the peace between
you.
*Kovrin walks off, heading a little upstage center, where he
stops and stands with his back to them.*

PESOTSKY

He's right, you know. A father's love is like our wild trees. It sometimes has a wild shape.

TANYA

Did you really tell Orlov to drown himself?

PESOTSKY

I did.

Gathering the tray of food, he rises, and she rises with him as they prepare to go.

TANYA

What if he does it?

PESOTSKY

Well, that would be a shock. Because for the first time in history, he would have done what he was told!

TANYA

You are a naughty man.

PESOTSKY

No, no, it's not possible. Poor Orlov. Drowned on orders.

They laugh and exit, never looking at Kovrin. Once they are gone, he turns to the audience.

KOVRIN

Good. They're laughing. It's a dear sound. Though their savagery was unnerving. The way it was directed so knowingly at its target. They needed me, until they didn't. And now I would like to get away. To go off in the woods, where I would find the trees. The animals. I would find silence. We all want people to be good and to love one another. But what if we aren't? What if we don't?

The lights have dimmed to evening, and he looks around.

Is it so dark so quickly? What time is it?

From off comes a chorus of feminine laughter.

And visitors already?

Looking around, puzzled.

Night already, and the guests have come for dinner. . . .

Sounds of the violin and singing voices rise up. They startle him and he listens, remembering.

That violin again, and they sing, but one can't quite understand . . .

The violin and voices continue, while he smiles at the audience.

I know what you're thinking. That serenade. Those voices. It must remind you of him just as it reminds me. And thinking of The Black Monk, we have to wonder where he is. In what country, over what far-off planet, does that optical absurdity travel now?

Without the slightest rustle, The Black Monk appears. He carries a long, staff-like walking stick.

THE BLACK MONK

Hello.

KOVRIN

Looks at him in amazement.

What are you doing here? And you're not moving or flying, but just standing. Such behavior is not correct according to the legend.

THE BLACK MONK

It does not matter, Kovrin. I have to tell you something: there is no legend.

KOVRIN

Of course there is.

THE BLACK MONK

No, the legend, the idea of the mirage, and I are all the products of your wild and overly active imagination.

KOVRIN

But the book that I read was explicit. It was very—

THE BLACK MONK

There is no book. The book that you keep looking for doesn't exist. I am a phantom.

KOVRIN

In what sense?

THE BLACK MONK

In the sense that I am a phantom.

KOVRIN

I hope you realize that you're saying that you don't actually exist.

THE BLACK MONK

Think what you like. However, I exist in your imagination, and your imagination is part of nature, therefore it must be admitted that, logically, by existing in your imagination, I exist in nature.

KOVRIN

But the way you appear so wise and intelligent, and your face is so highly expressive, you look as if you have in fact lived more than a thousand years. Could my imagination create such a phenomenon?

THE BLACK MONK

Apparently, it has.
He is clearly pleased.

KOVRIN

Why do you look at me with such delight?

THE BLACK MONK

Because you are one of the few on this earth about whom it can be said that God has touched you, so that you serve eternal truth. Your thoughts, your intentions, all your resourceful scholarship is sacred, because you are dedicated to the ideal, which is to say, to "the inspired" or in other words, "to all that is eternal."

KOVRIN
A second ago—you said I served "eternal truth."

THE BLACK MONK
I did.

KOVRIN
But we die.

THE BLACK MONK
Yes.

KOVRIN
We die.

THE BLACK MONK
Yes.

KOVRIN
But don't you see! Of what use is eternal truth to mankind if there's no eternal life?

THE BLACK MONK
But there is eternal life.

KOVRIN
For man? You're saying the human soul is immortal?

THE BLACK MONK
Of course. What awaits the human race is a blessed future. And the more people like you there are, the sooner that future will appear. You and others like you will bring humanity into contact with eternal truth hundreds of thousands of years ahead of what would have been possible without your effort. That is your great service. You embody God's grace, which at times can only arrive on earth through people.

KOVRIN

I see. And may I ask—what is the point of eternal life?

THE BLACK MONK

Enjoyment. Delight. Wonder. Happiness. The same as for any life. But eternal life gives knowledge, and since true knowledge brings true joy, one may see why it is said that "In the house of My Father there are many dwelling places . . ."

KOVRIN

If only you knew how encouraging it is for me to hear you say these things.

THE BLACK MONK

It should be very encouraging.

KOVRIN

It is. But already I worry that when you leave, which I'm sure you must—

THE BLACK MONK

Oh, yes.

KOVRIN

I worry I will be troubled by questions regarding your nature. If you're a phantom, and I'm talking to you, that means there's something wrong with me.

THE BLACK MONK

And what if it does?

KOVRIN

Well, then I'm mentally ill.

THE BLACK MONK

Why be troubled by that? If you are ill, it's because you give everything you have in order to do good. Think how you just helped

Tanya and her father. Could they have reconciled without you? And something else happened, didn't it, Kovrin? You discovered something.

KOVRIN

Yes.

THE BLACK MONK

You have always believed you could never love a strong, energetic woman. But you found that Tanya, when she was so unhappy, her melancholy shone through.

KOVRIN

In the flutter of her hand, I felt her nerves respond to my orphan spirit with an undeniable force.

THE BLACK MONK

If she'd asked you to give more, to give all, you would have given it. Of course you would have. You know you would have.

KOVRIN

Yes.

THE BLACK MONK

And if the time is coming when you must sacrifice all—to give up your health to your ideals, or to lose your life—what could be better? For one such as you, in whom grace has instilled a noble nature, there can be no higher hope!

KOVRIN

And yet if I'm mentally ill and I know it, how can I still believe in myself?

THE BLACK MONK

Consider the great men of history, Kovrin. Men who are revered by their civilizations. Do you know for a fact that they didn't see phantoms? Doesn't it seem that only simple people are healthy and normal? Doesn't it strike you that those who warn against ecstasy do so because they believe that human life is nothing beyond the physical? They believe only in the material, and so they are lost. They are lost in the present-day.

KOVRIN

In other words, you're saying they are spellbound by modern society.

THE BLACK MONK

Exactly!

KOVRIN

Still, I'm concerned that it was written by both the Greeks and Romans that *"Mens sana in corpore sano."*

THE BLACK MONK

But do you believe it? Does your experience tell you that a vigorous body guarantees a vigorous mind?

KOVRIN

Well, no.

THE BLACK MONK

Of course not. Because not every thing written down by even the Greeks and Romans is correct.

He gives a wild, incantatory howl.

Delirium! Exaltation!

Again he demonstrates with a wild sound.

Euphoria! These are virtues that define the prophets, that mark the poets, that proclaim the visionary martyrs. Such men must always stand opposed to the animal side of human life, whose single concern is to placate the gross appetites. Take my word for it, if you want to be ordinary, conform to your neighbor and you will remain now and forever a nonentity.

KOVRIN

It's so strange, the way you repeat what has come into my own mind so often. That's something that I think all the time.

THE BLACK MONK

Of course you do.

KOVRIN

I know. It's as if you've overheard my hidden, my innermost thoughts. But let's not talk about me. When you say "eternal truth," what is the concept behind your words?

When The Black Monk does not answer, Kovrin grows wary.
What I mean is, what would it consist of? Or is that an impertinent question?

The Black Monk starts to moves away.
I'm sorry if I— Are you going?

THE BLACK MONK

Yes.

KOVRIN

Following.
But at least answer my last question. I'm sorry to insist, but . . . I can no longer distinguish your face. Your head and arms seem to have become the evening twilight.

THE BLACK MONK

I'm dissolving.

And The Black Monk is gone, leaving Kovrin alone.

KOVRIN

It's over. It can't be.

He looks to the place where The Black Monk stood.
But it is. He's gone.

To the audience.
And yet his message was inspiring, wasn't it?

Moving down onto the miniature thrust.

To find myself recognized among the ranks of those who serve eternal truth, those who would raise humanity up and keep people from centuries of needless suffering! Yes, he flattered me. I know. But when I remember how hard I have worked, when I remember every book I've read, and paper I've memorized, all that I've studied and taught, I feel there is truth in his words. Yes, he flattered me. But it was not my vanity. Rather, he flattered my soul. He gave me a way to—

> *Tanya appears, walking toward him. Kovrin, overflowing with the rapturous effects of his vision, sees her from that blissful vantage.*

TANYA

Are you here? Doing what? You're always running off!

KOVRIN

Tanya. Tanya!

TANYA

I've been searching all over for you. I wanted to—
> *Approaching, staring at him.*
Your face is all shiny, your eyes—Are those tears?

KOVRIN

I don't know. I'm happy.

TANYA

Happy, but weeping. You are so strange, Andryusha. What's wrong?

KOVRIN

Nothing. Oh, Tanya, I see—you are an exceptional, wonderful creature.
> *Unable to look away, as if she is miraculous.*
And I'm so happy you're here. I love seeing you. I love seeing you, Tanya. The way we meet each morning in some room or some field, over and over, ten times a day we pass in the hall, or I hear you so that I know you're always near—always about to appear—

these moments have become each one a treasure to me—they are indispensable to my soul, to my breath, so that I cannot imagine surviving without them. Without you. Once I go back to my home in the city, what will I do?

TANYA
Kovrin, you're so excited. You should calm down.

KOVRIN
I know, I know, but what will I do?

TANYA
Laughing, uncomfortable, almost dizzy.
You'll manage just fine, Kovrin. You'll forget all about us in a matter of days. Once you're back with your fancy friends in the big city and—

KOVRIN
Tanya, stop! I won't hear it. I'll take you with me. Will you come with me? Will you be mine?

TANYA
What?

KOVRIN
Marry me. Please. This is our life, our life.

TANYA
Trying to laugh but failing.
Stop now. What are you saying? That's mean. Don't tease me. I don't like it.

KOVRIN
He kneels before her.
Marry me, marry me. I'm asking you please. I love you and I am accustomed to loving you. I will perish without it—without love. You know this is true.

TANYA
Go with you? Do you mean it?

KOVRIN
So that we can live as we should. So you can be as you dreamed—
confident and clever.

TANYA
I never thought of this.
    Moving off from him.
Never.

KOVRIN
But you did.

TANYA
What's happening to me!
    Looking around, as if fearful, and then to him.
I never thought of it!

KOVRIN
I want a love that will overwhelm me, Tanya, a love that will seize
and consume me, and you—you can give me such a love.

TANYA
Kovrin, I feel so strange. I feel . . . old. Suddenly, old.

KOVRIN
No.

TANYA
It's as if I've aged years and years.
    Starting to sink to the floor, her face bowed.

KOVRIN
No.

TANYA

But it is, Kovrin.
> *Still keeping her face averted.*

Please. What do you see?

KOVRIN

Let me look. Let me see.
> *Gently he turns her and gazes into her eyes, and what he sees is amazing.*

You're beautiful. Oh. Yes. Yes.
> *To the audience.*

How lovely she is!
> *He cradles her.*

BLACKOUT

ACT TWO

SCENE ONE

*Alone, outdoors, the trees in bloom, Pesotsky, wearing
his coat, paces.*

PESOTSKY

What do they mean, a wedding? What do they mean?
He rings a servant bell.
Here, here!!
Ringing.
No, no, no. We haven't the time!
As Orlov enters.
Harness the racing *droshky* as fast as you can. I must have it now—
this very second!

ORLOV

Sir, your daughter is looking for you.

PESOTSKY

No, no, we haven't the time! My racing *droshky* now!
*He's chasing Orlov off as Tanya enters, carrying a large,
brightly colored blanket.*

TANYA

Father, there you are. What are you doing out here? I need you to
come and—

PESOTSKY

No, no, I haven't the time!

TANYA

But the seamstresses are waiting for you! All of them. We need
your approval on my wedding dress, Father.

PESOTSKY
Dresses? Who can think of dresses when the peaches and plums
are ripe in the hothouse? They will rot if they are not packed and
shipped off to Moscow without delay. The task is gigantic, over-
whelming, and—

ORLOV
Sir, your *droshky* is ready.

PESOTSKY
Fine. Thank God for it.
Heading off.

TANYA
But Father, where are you going?! The guests are soon to arrive.

PESOTSKY
What guests?

TANYA
The guests for the party. Nadia and Mikhail and Yakov.
They'll be—

PESOTSKY
No, no. I haven't time.
He marches off, leaving her with Orlov.

TANYA
But we invited them!
Frazzled, she looks about.
Any talk of the wedding sends him racing off. Did you see, Orlov,
how he snorted and how deeply he pulled his cap down over his
ears? Where is he going?

ORLOV
It's not mine to know, little mistress.

TANYA
Watching Pesotsky drive off.
Look how he lashes the horses. Oh, I know his mood. I know his thoughts. With so much work in the orchard, my wedding and everything about it is a terrible nuisance to him. I'm a burden, everything—
And so the guests walk in—Mikhail and Nadia and Yakov—dressed for a party.

MIKHAIL
Hello. We're here. Yegor Semyonitch just went galloping off.

YAKOV
I think he waved to us. Or at least he gestured in our direction.

TANYA
You've arrived.

NADIA
This is what occurs when you invite people to dinner, Tanya. They arrive!

MIKHAIL
Punctual as the devil.
They laugh, as Tanya agrees to greet them as a competent hostess.

TANYA
Excuse me, forgive me.
Taking Yakov's hands.
Forgive us, Yakov.
And then to them all, attempting hugs, kisses.
Father's overwrought. And I am, too. He can't— He's gone, I don't know where.
Trying to spread the blanket on the ground for a picnic, as the guests help her.

Well, what are we to do—and so he runs away. And I, too, want nothing to do with any of it. Like my father, I want to—
>*Breaking down, she flees.*

Forgive me.
>*The guests look off after her, then finish arranging the blanket.*

MIKHAIL
Well, now everyone's gone.

NADIA
The guests are present but the hosts have flown the coop.

ORLOV
They do this.

MIKHAIL
What's that, Orlov?

YAKOV
They do what?
>*They settle down on the blanket.*

NADIA
Yes, yes, tell us what you know.

ORLOV
The master bellows and gallops about from here to there. If it's not this, it's that. At the same time, the mistress screams and runs to her room, where she cries all day. Do you want me to go get the tea?

NADIA
By all means, but first—does this happen often?

ORLOV
Well, what is often?

NADIA
I'm sorry. What?

YAKOV
The man would know "what is often," Nadia? In the name of clarity, he will not start without an approved vocabulary.

NADIA
Well, then as just witnessed by us all, the actions of the pair of them—has it happened before?

ORLOV
Yes, madame.

NADIA
Teasing and playful.
And this example, as far as you know, is it the first today?

ORLOV
Yes, but twice yesterday. After breakfast, and again midafternoon.

MIKHAIL
Twice yesterday. Once today. I would say it sounds quite a bit like "often."

YAKOV
I'm wondering, Orlov, might we have a bottle of wine instead of tea?

NADIA
And where is Kovrin in all of this?

ORLOV
With his books. He works and smiles and kisses her. She cries, he laughs. The master leaps into his *droshky* and races off.
Tanya returns bearing a bowl of apples.

TANYA

I'm sorry. Forgive me. Oh, thank you for coming.

NADIA

Hello, hello.

Nadia hurries to her and they hug. Tanya greets them all again with kisses, hugs.

MIKHAIL

Darling, Tanya.

YAKOV

We knew you'd return. How are you?

TANYA

You must forgive me. I can no longer trust or explain myself. I'm simply overcome by things. I have no idea what they are or why they occur. They are just little storms that come and go.

MIKHAIL

Might I suggest that you are suffering from the problem of happiness?

NADIA

Yes. And I think love.

YAKOV

A tricky pair.

TANYA

Well, I warn you against them, for they have caught me unprepared.

NADIA

And yet Tanya, though you say "unprepared," I remember eating bread and jam in the sun with you not that long ago—we were teenaged girls sitting by the river, when utterly unprovoked—

Turning to the others..

—she announced that she and Kovrin would someday marry.

TANYA

I never did.

NADIA

Of course you did, Tanya. The sun was up, the jam was blueberry.

TANYA

Never.
Orlov returns with a tray of wine and glasses.

MIKHAIL

Ah, yes, Orlov. Good.
To Tanya.
We dared request wine on our own authority.
Pouring the wine.

TANYA

It never happened, Nadia.

NADIA

Tanya, you may say "never" all you want, I cannot stop you; but I remember it emphatically.

TANYA

You do? You remember it?

YAKOV

"Emphatically," she says.

TANYA

Well, all right, then, I admit it. It's just too spooky. Did I know? Did I seek it? I can ask. I have asked, but don't know. And yet it happens. In less than two months we will marry and I'll travel to Moscow. And what I feel as I say these things, as I admit them, I

feel such joy I want to fly to the clouds and thank God face-to-face. I will go away from my childhood home—
> *On comes one of those little storms of feeling.*

I will leave my father and everything I have ever known and go off with Andryusha—
> *Tears are taking over*

—even though I'm a nonentity. Because I am unworthy of Kovrin. I've no right to so great a man. No right at all.
> *Kovrin strolls in, a glass of wine in his hands.*

NADIA
Ohhhhhhh.
> *Holding Tanya to console her.*

TANYA
Ohhhh, what is wrong with me, Nadia?

YAKOV
Ahhh, Kovrin, help. Your bride-to-be seems to be falling to smithereens.

KOVRIN
So there she goes. Tears again.
> *Hastening to Tanya.*

No doubt the subject was love. And marriage. And me.
> *Hugging Tanya.*

Am I the only happy one? Ahhh. Well.
> *He smiles at the others.*

Hello, hello.
> *Just as Pesotsky marches in.*

PESOTSKY
Well, I'm back. Hello, my darling friends.

MIKHAIL
Yegor Semyonitch, we thought you were gone for the night.

PESOTSKY
No, no. Let me be honest. I have no idea where I was going. It was just a kind of wild exercise I had to have, who knows why. And then before I'd gotten a thousand yards peasants were in the road. Screaming that I must stop. Well, what was it you ask? I didn't want to know, and yet they told me. A sheep! Yes, a sheep was giving birth. And with their peasant brains making peasant reasons out of peasant thoughts they seemed to think I must witness these lambs' arrival on the earth. Do you know what I thought? No, thank you! And back I come, outracing them as I would run from a pack of devils.

NADIA
Newborn lambs? Really?

PESOTSKY
According to the peasants.

NADIA
Is it far? Let's go see them.

KOVRIN
Would you like to, Nadia?

MIKHAIL
Yes. Could we, Yegor Semyonitch?

PESOTSKY
If you must.
To Orlov.
But let Orlov go first and find out from the peasants how the sheep have fared.
To the others as Orlov hurries to go.
Let them at least separate the living lambs from the dead ones, and clean up the gore.
Then calling to Orlov, who is almost to the door.

But Orlov! First bring cheese and black bread and apples and pears.

>*Seeing Mikhail gesture with an empty wine bottle.*

And more wine. We have apples!

>*Calling after Orlov, who is now out the door.*

We have apples!

YAKOV

Yegor Semyonitch, your farm appears in splendid condition. As we drove in, the sight was thrilling.

MIKHAIL

Yes, yes. No matter what direction one looks something is growing.

>*Everyone settles on the blanket, sharing the wine.*

PESOTSKY

Well, I hope so, because the place is running me ragged. I charge around sunburned and panting and losing my temper. Here I am with peaches and plums ripe in the hothouse and it's already time to place the autumn orders for fruit and trees.

>*Orlov scurries in with two trays of food and wine, which he sets down before racing off.*

TANYA

And then just last week, hordes of caterpillars came, millions of them, all wanting to eat the—

PESOTSKY

>*Lying back beside the blanket to gaze at the sky.*

My God, they were hateful!

KOVRIN

Everyone, listen! Yegor Semyonitch and all the workers and even Tanya were all squashing caterpillars with their bare hands.

NADIA

With their bare hands?

KOVRIN

It was disgusting!

PESOTSKY

And tomorrow, with sales and shipping only half done, the work in the fields must begin. It's impossible.

KOVRIN

You should have heard him just last night.

PESOTSKY

Who?

KOVRIN

You. What you said when you came in the door.

PESOTSKY

No, no, that wasn't for anyone's ears but my own.

NADIA

What did he say?

PESOTSKY

Kovrin, that wasn't meant for you to hear, and it's most certainly not for this group.

NADIA

You must tell us, Kovrin, please!

KOVRIN

I was sitting, reading. In he comes, so covered in dust he looks like somebody just dropped him out of a passing coach and he tumbled in the door and—

PESOTSKY
Well, all right then! If we must. If I must.
Laughing.
But mind you, there's not a word of truth in it. However, if you must know, what I said was, "It's all tearing me to bits and I think I'm going to put a bullet through my brain."

TANYA
Oh, Papa, no; you didn't say that.

PESOTSKY
I'm afraid so.
He remains lying back, calmly, and everyone is quite amused.

MIKHAIL
Yegor Semyonitch, I know a less drastic solution.

PESOTSKY
Everyone, please! I wasn't serious.

MIKHAIL
Nevertheless. Let me suggest: move to Moscow. Sell the farm.

PESOTSKY
Give up the orchard, you're saying.

MIKHAIL
Precisely. Search out another enterprise. Better yet, enjoy yourself.

PESOTSKY
Give up the orchard, you're saying. How little you know, Mikhail Ivonovitch. For if ever I did as you advise, I would shoot myself for certain. Yes, yes, it's true—I must run around like a chicken with my head cut off. But if my heart could speak, here's what it would say. Thank God for it. Let everyone love the demands of their life as much as I do!
Orlov steps in.

ORLOV
Two lambs have been born, master. Two healthy lambs. Both of the two of them healthy.

NADIA
I want to go see them. Kovrin, let's go.

KOVRIN
Oh, yes, yes. Good.
Nadia grabs Kovrin's hand, and they head for the door.

MIKHAIL
I'll come.

KOVRIN
As Nadia drags him off.
Tanya, come along!

YAKOV
Going with Nadia and Kovrin.
Yes, let's go. Tanya, you don't want to miss them. Come on!
But Tanya lingers, gazing at her father, who lies there, eyes closed, hands behind his head, relaxed and sleepy in the sun.

TANYA
Father.

PESOTSKY
What?

TANYA
Why would you say such a thing?

PESOTSKY
No, no, little Tanya, let's not get stuck on nothing.

TANYA
Are you that unhappy?

PESOTSKY
Please. I told you it wasn't serious. It was just a tired man saying tired thoughts. What we say when we think we are alone belongs to us and no one else.
Now Yakov returns.

YAKOV
Tanya, we're getting left behind.
Moving in, he takes her by the hand.
If I may not marry you, at least I can walk you to the barn to see the lovely little lambs.

TANYA
Come with us, Father. I want your company.

PESOTSKY
The lambs are born, they're dear, they're darling, we slaughter them. I think I'll skip this little visit.

YAKOV
Clutching her hand, tugging to move her off.
Tanya. Baaaaaaaaaa, I say. Baaaaaaaa. I have your hand and you must come with me. Baaaaaaaaa!
Tanya goes with Yakov, and Pesotsky is left with only Orlov, who sits off to the side on a stool.

PESOTSKY
Yes, well. Baaaaaaaaa! Yakov.
He doesn't really need to look to see that Orlov is there.
You have daughters, Orlov.

ORLOV
Yes, sir. Three of them.

PESOTSKY
Andrei Vasilich Kovrin. Son-in-law. His mother died of consumption, you know, Orlov. That's a fact.

ORLOV
Yes, sir.

PESOTSKY
You did know that?
Sitting up, almost waking from a sleep.

ORLOV
No, sir.

PESOTSKY
Well, it's true. She was noble and intelligent. Kovrin looks like her. She wrote poetry and made wonderful sketches. Spoke five languages. Five. And well, too. Then died of consumption. I'm certain you see my thought.

ORLOV
Yes, sir.

PESOTSKY
Of course it concerns me. What if he's like her? Who wouldn't worry? And now they're marrying. They played here as children. Blood means a lot. It comes from the mother, you know. Such an illness. And yet, let no one forget that he has his master's degree! And his triumphs have barely begun. One day we will all be proud to have known him. Happy to be able to claim that we—
Tanya, with a kind of wail, comes running in.
Tanya, what is it?

TANYA
She's startled to see him.
Nothing, no, no. I'm sorry.

PESOTSKY
Nothing, you say, after flying in here as if—

TANYA
Father, please, I beg you. I forbid you.
Backing away.
Do not interrogate me!
Kovrin arrives, worried, seeking her.

KOVRIN
Tanya!

PESOTSKY
Kovrin, yes. Please, you see to her. If you dare. She is beyond me.
Which is only to be expected, I know, given—I don't know what.
But let me say it anyway! Given—
He strides off.
EVERYTHING! EVERYTHING!
*Kovrin approaches Tanya, who has flung herself to the
ground.*

KOVRIN
Tanya, my sweet one, my darling, what is it?

TANYA
Forgive me. It's so shameful. So petty. So pitiful. It's all so sad.

KOVRIN
No, no, no.
He tries to hold her, and she gives in a little.

TANYA
But it is! The guests arrive and it seems to me that you are the
most wonderful man in the room. All the women are in love with
you; they envy me. And my heart fills with delight, and pride, as if
I've conquered the world. But then Nadia comes up to you, I see
her smile and you say something, and her eyes gleam, looking at

you, and you laugh, you take her hand. I can't stand it! It's so shameful.

> *Now she relaxes a little in his arms, her head against his chest as she gazes off, and he, listening, follows her gaze with his own.*

People play cards. They plow fields. They go to the city or on a picnic. They fight duels and gamble away fortunes. Why? Why?

> *Yakov, Nadia, Mikhail return to find this embrace.*

NADIA
Ohhhh, look at them.

YAKOV
I was afraid we would find them like this.

NADIA
Yakov, you must give up all hope.

YAKOV
It is obvious, and so I see it.

> *Trailing the guests is The Black Monk. He walks in as if he is one of them, only a step or so back.*

MIKHAIL
Weren't the lambs adorable, Tanya?

NADIA
They were so sweet.

TANYA
They were very sweet. Little lambs, little lambs.

> *Kovrin, fixated on The Black Monk, moves toward him.*

KOVRIN
> *To audience.*

Look who's here—look who has arrived. I was hoping he might show up.

To The Black Monk.
Hello. Hello!

PESOTSKY
*Entering from behind The Black Monk so that it seems
Kovrin is talking to him.*
Hello!

KOVRIN
To Pesotsky.
Hello!
To the audience.
I'll try to turn the conversation to a topic that will interest him.
Something he can enjoy hearing us talk about. So he doesn't feel
left out!
Loudly.
Love only pours fuel on the fire!

MIKHAIL
What's that, Kovrin?

KOVRIN
I'm speaking of love and the way it fuels everything in life. I love
Tanya, and I meet with her, I kiss her, I declare my love, and then
with that same feeling of happiness and full of lofty enthusiasm I
go to my work. I take up my writing or some book of research.
This is what I know—all love is one, all one, and there are paths
for us chosen by God. And this path gives my work a singular
meaning. For I've come to believe that there are men who, once
they have consecrated themselves to the service of the ideal, they
are not left alone in their work, but they are visited by holy and
special assistance.
*Kovrin has ended face-to-face with The Black Monk, who
has listened and approved and smiled.*

PESOTSKY
Kovrin, to whom do you speak?

KOVRIN
Turning back to them all.
Well, to everyone! Everyone!
And then he moves past The Black Monk to Tanya.
But mainly, and most importantly, to Tanya.
He takes Tanya in his arms and, holding her tight, kisses her, a long, loving kiss, and everyone watches and is charmed.

ORLOV
Rising.
Dinner is ready!

YAKOV
At last. I'm starving.

NADIA
Not a minute too soon. I only hope they're not serving lamb.
Laughing, they all start to go.

MIKHAIL
Please, no lamb!

NADIA
And no caterpillars.
But Pesotsky rings a servant bell and stops them.

PESOTSKY
But one minute, my wonderful friends. Please, my darling guests. Lambs! Sunburn! Tears! Caterpillars! Racing here, racing there, and suddenly it's time to eat. What next? Well, night, and sleep. And so on, as unbeknownst to us, it all goes on until suddenly it will be upon us—the day of the wedding. No doubt, our revelry will be loud, and it will proceed for days and days, I guarantee it. Here and now I pledge three thousand rubles to be given over for the finest wines and most remarkable food I can transport from Moscow. And to our perfect music we will add our own joyous

noise and our many clamorous toasts, the first of which I make
right now.

> *Raising his glass.*

To my precious Tanya and my beloved and almost-son, Andrei
Vasilich. May the love of God and the God of Love be in your
hearts from this day to the next, and so on and etcetera, and what's
more, I say, "forever!"

> *He toasts, they all toast and drink.*

ALL

Forever!

> *Music. Lights. And as the guests and Pesotsky go,*
> *Tanya stands in narrowing light, and snow begins to*
> *fall on her.*

SCENE TWO

> *Music. Night. Sound of wind. Snow falls on Tanya, then*
> *diminishes as she and Kovrin are found undressing near a*
> *large bed in Kovrin's Moscow apartment. A chair stands*
> *just off the downstage right foot of the bed. They both*
> *are getting ready for bed.*

TANYA

Moscow is so cold!

KOVRIN

Well, yes. Soon you can bundle up.

TANYA

Aren't you freezing?

KOVRIN

Hurry and burrow under the blankets.

TANYA

I'm freezing in this city!

KOVRIN

You behave as if winters in the countryside are comfortable. It's all one icy Russia. No more here than anywhere else.

TANYA

In the countryside we have large fireplaces and blazing fires.

KOVRIN

Tanya, we have fireplaces. We have fires.

TANYA

Not as big.

KOVRIN

You're getting all worked up over nothing.

TANYA

I have a headache.

KOVRIN

Again? Poor Tanya.

TANYA

Are you smiling? Does my headache amuse you?

KOVRIN

No, no. It's just—I have no idea. I'm just smiling. I'm happy.
He is putting on a robe, as Tanya, shivering, climbs into bed.

TANYA

It's this city and living in it. The buildings keep in the cold. They're fortresses made of blocks of frozen stone.
He helps her under the covers, adds a blanket.

I grow less accustomed to it the longer I live here. The harder I try to adjust, the more I become a stranger.
>*She waits for him.*
Please come to bed, too.

KOVRIN
I must read a while. But I'll be near.
>*Settling into the chair.*
I'll be right here.

TANYA
Reading.

KOVRIN
Yes.

TANYA
Well, if you have no choice. Goodnight.

KOVRIN
Goodnight, dear Tanya.

TANYA
Goodnight, my husband.

KOVRIN
Goodnight, my wife.
>*Eager to read, he smiles to the audience, gestures with the book.*
Nothing too demanding. A French novel.
>*He reads, sharing with the audience.*
"As Jacques turned the corner, he saw the shadow wavering in the window one floor above his own small apartment. He knew that Andre was up there in the candlelight, laboring on his great work, and Jacques felt lost and hopeless, suddenly, as if he had been flung from a moving coach by people who no longer thought him interesting."

Looking out to the audience.
Poor Jacques.

TANYA
Cantankerous and without vegetables.
   Sound asleep, she lies on her back, propped up on pillows.

KOVRIN
What?

TANYA
That horse is too big for the door.

KOVRIN
Well, listen to that. And she's sound asleep.
   The clock chimes: gong. Gong. Gong.

TANYA
   Asleep.
No, no, not that hat!

KOVRIN
Three o'clock, already?
   Rising, moving to the bed, blowing out the candle.
Perhaps I should try to sleep a bit.
   He settles in bed.

TANYA
   Asleep.
If they don't drop it . . . we can all have proper grammar.

KOVRIN
Listen to her. I wonder who is dropping what.
   Shifting, settling, closing his eyes.
I'll just close my eyes . . . and then . . . perhaps . . .

TANYA

No one knows what kind of shoes to give the chickens!

KOVRIN

Goodness.
Looking at her, a little annoyed.
Is she going to keep this up?
The clock chimes once: gong.
Another half an hour already.

TANYA
Asleep.
The cows, the cows, the . . .

KOVRIN

This is hopeless
Sitting up.
Utterly hopeless.

TANYA

Tell the cows I am so sorry. . . .

KOVRIN

With her mumbling and carrying on, I'll never— Where's my book? After all, I left poor Jacques in such an unhappy state. Perhaps if I read and find out what happened to him, I'll be able to . . . calm my thoughts.
He is lighting a candle, and in the candlelight, The Black Monk is revealed upstage.

THE BLACK MONK

But why are you agitated about *that,* Kovrin? You must tell me why you're letting such a trivial subject overtake your mind.

KOVRIN

I'm not really so agitated.

THE BLACK MONK
I feel that you are. And of all things? Fame, Kovrin. Fame.

KOVRIN
You're right. But I assume it's the fact that I was just reading this French novel, and in it there's a young man, Jacques, a novice scholar, and he behaves stupidly. He wastes his talent in frustration and bitterness, because he pines for fame. In the way other young men pine for love, this Jacques longs for fame. And I was thinking that I don't understand such a longing. It bewilders me.

THE BLACK MONK
Well, of course it does. You're intelligent and wise, and so indifferent to fame.

KOVRIN
I think it's a trifle, like a toy.

THE BLACK MONK
What could fame possibly offer that you might want? To have your name shouted about and then cut into your gravestone only to have Time blot it out, and then to blot out the inscription, and then wipe out even the dates, and finally to obliterate even the stone itself. Where's the appeal in that? Billions of people have walked the earth since the beginning of time, but thank heavens only a few are remembered. Don't you agree?

KOVRIN
Yes, I do. Though some might find your idea sad, it reflects my feelings exactly. There's no reason to remember anyone.

TANYA
Asleep.
It's time for everyone to raise all of their . . . umbrellas.
> *The clock strikes four. Gong. Gong. Gong. Gong. And as the gongs ring, The Black Monk moves down to the foot of the bed.*

KOVRIN

But let's talk about something else. Happiness, for example. I want to talk about happiness. What is it, and is it dangerous?

THE BLACK MONK

You are aware that it's now four o'clock in the morning.

KOVRIN

Yes, yes, but I have no interest in sleep.
Kovrin moves close to The Black Monk.

THE BLACK MONK

Your enthusiasm is deeply inspiring.

KOVRIN

I want to be honest. This is not altogether theoretical. Because I'm worried. In ancient times there was a man—Policrates. Now I'm not worried about Policrates, but myself. Policrates was so happy he grew frightened of his own happiness. I think that I'm like him. Happy, but too happy. I find my happiness disturbing. It drowns out all other feelings. From morning till night I have no idea what sadness is, or boredom. Right now, I am suffering from insomnia, but I remain happy. I am very happy right now. Seriously, I'm beginning to wonder.

THE BLACK MONK

Well, Kovrin, the world is full of wonder.

TANYA
Asleep.
Has anyone seen my warm gray mittens?
Startled, Kovrin and The Black Monk look at Tanya, who turns over onto her side, still asleep.
My hands are old. . . .

KOVRIN
Back to The Black Monk.
No, no, I mean I'm beginning to wonder if I should worry.

THE BLACK MONK
On that point, I say no. Not at all, because—

KOVRIN
Would you mind if I wrote some of this down?
Kovrin reaches for his notebook and a pen.

THE BLACK MONK
That might be prudent. Just some notes for later reference. But hurry.

KOVRIN
Why?

THE BLACK MONK
Pacing, speaking, dictating.
I'm excited. As I was about to say—why should mankind view joy as an unnatural state when it is in fact their right? As a man develops his intellectual and moral gifts, he becomes free in a way that brings true pleasure. Think of Buddha, Pythagoras, the great Shakespeare—they all experienced joy. And remember what the Apostle says—

KOVRIN
I know, I know.

THE BLACK MONK
"Rejoice and be happy."
Settles in the chair at the foot of the bed.

KOVRIN
But I remain concerned. I have to tell you. I think of Policrates and how he tried to barter with his gods—he had gods, and he

tried to appease them by giving them his most treasured ring. It was a kind of bribe. And what I'm worried about is—what if my gods grow angry, suddenly?

Trying to joke a little.

What if they take away my comforts? What if they force me to go cold and hungry?

Behind Kovrin, Tanya wakes up. She looks at Kovrin in astonishment. He is addressing The Black Monk, arguing, enjoying himself.

THE BLACK MONK
You would do well. Cold and hungry would suit you.

KOVRIN
What? No, no, no. I don't think so.

THE BLACK MONK
But you have never tried them, and so your opinion is unfounded.

KOVRIN
I feel a strong aversion. Untested, I have my conviction.

Happily arguing.

No, no. I'll leave that to you. Vagabond that you are. Cold and hungry might suit the likes of you, roaming the universe as you do. Do you recommend it because you've tried it? Or are you suggesting that you might teach me? Would you?

TANYA
Andryusha, who are you talking to?

KOVRIN
What?

He looks at her.

TANYA
Andryusha! There's no one here and you're talking.

KOVRIN

What?

The Black Monk raises his finger to his lips.

THE BLACK MONK

Shhhhhhhhhh!

Kovrin looks at The Black Monk, and then at Tanya.

TANYA

Ohhhh, Andryusha, forgive me, but I've noticed things. Father, too, has seen them, my darling, the both of us have worried that something—that your great mind is troubled. That your soul—

KOVRIN

You see no one?

TANYA

No, no. Look. Where?

KOVRIN

Well, of course, it's nothing, Tanya, nothing.

Trembling, moving to the bed.

Not that I—It's true that I'm not feeling well. It's as if I'm wandering, searching, I suppose, but I feel there is a destination, and yet it doesn't—I don't . . .

TANYA

We've noticed things for a while now. We both did, but we—

KOVRIN

"We," Tanya? We who?

TANYA

Father and me. We. As I just said, and—

KOVRIN
Oh, yes, yes—you and Father. We.

TANYA
You talk to yourself, you smile strangely.

KOVRIN
No, not to myself.

THE BLACK MONK
SHHHHHHH!

TANYA
Yes. To yourself. Not to me. You don't sleep. You're up all night talking to empty chairs!

KOVRIN
Well, enough of this.
Looking around, he rises, starts to dress.

TANYA
It's true what I'm saying.

KOVRIN
Suddenly very officious.
Well, it is, or it isn't.
Very much the professor.
Nevertheless, I say, "Enough!"

TANYA
Calling off to another room.
Father, Father!

KOVRIN
Don't call him! This is for you! For us. Husband and wife.
He keeps dressing, and it seems he will tell her a little to keep her from calling again.

I will say *perhaps* I have felt . . . I don't know what to call it? What shall I call it?
> *Following his example, Tanya begins getting dressed.*

TANYA
Just don't be afraid, Andryusha, don't be afraid.

KOVRIN
But I am. That's what I'll call it. That's what it is. I'm afraid. I'm very afraid.
> *His mood is changing, as he moves to sit on the foot of the bed to put on his shoes.*
And . . . why are we getting dressed?

TANYA
What?

KOVRIN
We are getting dressed. Why?

TANYA
Well, you were.

KOVRIN
Yes, yes. I am.
> *Working on his shoes.*
I see that. And you are, too.

TANYA
You started, and I— Well, you started, so I started—

KOVRIN
I asked, "Why? Why?"

TANYA
You started, so I started.
> *Still dressing.*

KOVRIN

But I have no idea why!

TANYA

I think it's a good idea, though.
Joining him at the foot of the bed, she starts to put on her shoes.

KOVRIN

Is it? All right, then let's do it. Let's dress.
Finishing his shoes.
Are we late for something?

TANYA

No, no. But we're up. I couldn't go back to sleep.

KOVRIN

I didn't sleep at all. I never sleep. You talk in your sleep.

TANYA

Grabbing a scarf, she shows it to him.
Shall I wear this?

KOVRIN

Do you like it?

TANYA

I do.

KOVRIN

Yes, yes. Then wear it. Wear it, please.
As he helps her put the scarf around her shoulders, they slowly stand.
Only now do I understand what my conversations with The Black Monk mean.

THE BLACK MONK
SHHHHHHHHH!

KOVRIN
Looking at us, hearing you, seeing you, Tanya, I understand what
my conversations with The Black Monk mean.

TANYA
Good, good, what do they mean?

KOVRIN
I think that they—I want to be precise and they—

TANYA
What black monk? There is no black monk!

KOVRIN
But there is!
Staring at The Black Monk and telling her.
Look!
Asking the audience.
Look!
Pesotsky enters; he wears a robe.

PESOTSKY
What is it? What's going on in here?

TANYA
Moving toward her father.
Don't be afraid, Papa, it will all pass. . . .

PESOTSKY
You're trembling. Tanya, my darling. Do you have a fever?

KOVRIN
Hello, Yegor Semyonitch. What are you doing here?

PESOTSKY
To Tanya.
What's he saying?
To Kovrin.
I'm your houseguest! For heaven's sake, I think you know that.

KOVRIN
Oh, yes.
Striding up to Pesotsky.
I must have forgotten.
Triumphant.
But now I remember.

PESOTSKY
Well, it's of no matter whether you do or don't, because I am here either way.

KOVRIN
You must congratulate me!

TANYA
It will all pass.

PESOTSKY
Yes, yes! I don't understand! What will pass?

KOVRIN
Yegor Semyonitch, congratulate me!

PESOTSKY
Congratulate you? Oh. Good. Wonderful! But why? I don't know what you're talking about.

TANYA
Papa, please, don't scold him! It has come, but it will pass.

PESOTSKY
Why are you all dressed? Where are you going? What is all this?

KOVRIN
Sitting.
Tanya, make him congratulate me!
And leaping up, he knocks the chair over.

PESOTSKY
All right, all right! I congratulate you, but, if you don't mind, if it's not too much bother—would you tell me why?

KOVRIN
Because, Yegor Semyonitch, apparently, I am insane! It would seem—if the truth be told, I am mad. I have lost my mind!

PESOTSKY
Oh! Oh! It has come.
To Tanya.
I'm so sorry my darling daughter. It has come as we feared, and our sorrow cannot change it. We must go. You're right. You're all ready, but I am not.
He rushes off.

KOVRIN
What's he doing? Where's he going? Yegor Semyonitch!

TANYA
We are dressed. He must get dressed.

KOVRIN
Yes, yes.
A servant bell rings loudly in another room.
Are we going somewhere?

TANYA

We've spoken to doctors, my darling. Father and I both. We've
been so worried. They're wonderful men. Wonderful men of sci-
ence. Educated men, like yourself.

As she hands him his overcoat.

KOVRIN

What men?

TANYA

We went seeking advice, seeking their excellent counsel, all the
while praying that such a moment as this would not come.

Pesotsky returns, wearing a big boot on one foot, carrying a
second boot, dragging his overcoat to put on over his robe,
and marching past The Black Monk, who they bustle
around and past, as he stands in their midst.

PESOTSKY

Are you telling him? These are excellent men—maestros—virtuo-
sos. The finest in their field. No effort will be spared on your
behalf. I made certain of that. You can rest assured. They understand such things.

Pulling the second boot on.

KOVRIN

What things?

TANYA

They know all about you.

KOVRIN

Is this because of The Black Monk? The things that I said.

PESOTSKY

No, no.

Two peasant men enter, looking cranky and tired, carrying
blankets.

KOVRIN
Because there is no need.

TANYA
No, my darling. It's not that.

PESOTSKY
To the peasant men.
You will assist Andrei Vasilich please.
*The peasant men move up to Kovrin. They put the coat on
him, bundle him up.*

PESOTSKY
Yes, yes, what a clear bright night for a carriage ride through the
sparkle of our Moscow streets.
*The peasant men are now on either side of Kovrin, who
stands stiffly, as they take hold of him, firmly.*
Come now. Come now, my boy. The dear white moon will guide us.
*The peasant men move him toward the door, everyone very
formal, very civilized, though he is being compelled.*

KOVRIN
Frightened, but with bravado.
Of course, of course. But there is no black monk. So you see. You
understand. There is no black monk. No black monk anywhere—
not flying or standing still! No book! No legend! No, no, no. Certainly not. What more can I say?
*Reassuringly, looking back to Pesotsky and Tanya, who
wait and follow him out.*
Yegor Semyonitch—Tanya, my wife—I saw nothing. Nothing at all.
*Pesotsky and Tanya follow, almost as if they are a couple at
a wedding or a funeral, leaving The Black Monk alone.
Then he, too, departs. Orlov enters. Perhaps Orlov and The
Black Monk pass each other, or, as one goes, the other
enters from the opposite direction. Orlov sets down a small
table and arranges the chair. Kovrin comes in.*

SCENE THREE

Borissovka: Kovrin stands by the chair, the table. Then he sits. Tanya enters from one direction, Pesotsky from another. Tanya carries a tray with a teapot and tea settings.

TANYA
We're going to have some tea. Would you care for some tea, Darling?

PESOTSKY
You missed a splendid service. The priest gave a fine sermon.

TANYA
He has a lovely singing voice.

PESOTSKY
God's gift. All in all, inspiring. I find Elijah's Day a very inspiring feast day, don't you, Kovrin? Very inspiring. And I have to tell you he took notice of your departure. But then the way you just stood up and walked off—who could miss it. I for one think you made a mistake. He's a very intelligent fellow, that priest, and from the little he had to say to me, I gathered he'd been hoping to engage you in some kind of theological discussion.
Silence.

TANYA
Where did you go on your walk? I hope you spent some time in the garden. It's in such a beautiful phase right now. Aren't the lilies glorious?

KOVRIN
I have no idea.

TANYA
Oh, you must.

KOVRIN
Perhaps I must, but I don't.

TANYA
How could you fail to notice?

KOVRIN
I don't know. But I have.

PESOTSKY
So where did you walk? What did you see?

KOVRIN
Nothing.

PESOTSKY
Impossible. You must have seen something! Or was your full ac-
complishment wandering around oblivious?

KOVRIN
You want to know where I walked? The mystery is solved. I
went to the river. I looked down at the water. I looked up at the
trees that just last year found me so joyful. Only today, with my
face pale, my heart dead in my chest, they no longer knew who I
was.

PESOTSKY
Or, might I suggest, they did not recognize you because they are
trees. And trees do not recognize anyone.

TANYA
Hoping to lighten the moment.
Except for you, Father. After all your devotion, I'm sure they
know you.

PESOTSKY

No. They are trees. It is enough that I know them.

KOVRIN

I crossed the bridge, and looked into that field where last summer there was rye, and I thought how much better it would've been for me to have fallen into a black hole in the earth than to allow you to bundle me up that night and hand me over to those doctors and their treatment. Get rest. Work only two hours a day. Drink milk. Never drink wine. Never smoke cigars. I stood for some twenty minutes looking, waiting until the sun began to set. A red glow covered the field, and then I had an idea.

TANYA

Oh?

KOVRIN

You're probably wondering what it is.

PESOTSKY

Of course we are. You are our son and husband.

KOVRIN

Though I am her husband, those dear souls to whom I am son are in the grave.

PESOTSKY

Fine. Answer me coldly, and when you look at me let it be with mockery. Hatred. Fine. I'm all for it.
He moves near Kovrin, pacing.
Mock me if it pleases you. It's nothing to me. As long as you get well. If it helps in your treatment, I'm at your disposal. Beleaguer me! I feel no guilt for my actions taken to help you.
Turning to leave.
What I have done, any man would do.
Pesotsky walks away, and when he is gone, Tanya moves near Kovrin.

TANYA
Why are you so unfair to him? He cares so much, he is so good!

KOVRIN
He isn't good. He is at best good-natured. Yes, perhaps he's good-
natured with a well-fed, piggish kind of optimism that I find disgusting.

TANYA
So you hate him. All right. But when he tells you he feels no guilt
about what's happened to you, don't believe him. He's cherished
you all his life. You should know that during the service at church
he was crying.
Just then Kovrin sees Orlov and calls to him.

KOVRIN
You there! Come here!

TANYA
It's time that you drink your milk, Kovrin.

KOVRIN
Well, where is it?
As Orlov hurries over.

TANYA
Do you want Orlov to get it?

KOVRIN
No. You get it. Go get my milk.
And then to Orlov.
And you. There are three boxes on the desk in my room.

TANYA
Are you thinking of working?

KOVRIN

I told you I had an idea. A wonderful, exciting idea. A liberating idea. It's an inspiring idea.

TANYA

Oh, good. Good. But don't work too hard.

KOVRIN

I'll be very careful. But I need my milk.
Tanya hurries off, and Kovrin turns to Orlov.
I said bring the boxes!

ORLOV

You want me to bring the boxes? Sir? Bring them here to you, sir?

KOVRIN

Yes, here to me! You idiot!
Orlov starts off, but Kovrin gestures to stop him.
Come back, come back.
Orlov halts, and Kovrin moves to him, uses a low voice.
Bring some wine and a fine cigar.

ORLOV

If you say so, sir.

KOVRIN

I did say so. Shall I say it again?

ORLOV

No, sir.
As Orlov hurries off, Pesotsky appears, returning from another direction.

PESOTSKY

Good luck. She's gone. Because I must be candid. It is my way. People say it about me—he is candid—and I am. This can't go on.

Don't you see how our Tanya can no longer enjoy a single moment of her day? This morning, for breakfast, she ate nothing. Not a crumb. She doesn't sleep. Whole nights go by. Just yesterday, she was so exhausted she lay on the couch looking sick and downcast from lunch until evening. And you should know that at church she was crying.

KOVRIN

Really. Tanya was crying at church.

> *Tanya returns with a glass and a large pitcher of milk, and Kovrin moves toward her as she places the milk on the table.*

How lucky was Buddha, and Pythagoras, and the great Shakespeare, all wise, happy and daring men, but mainly lucky that their relatives and doctors did not cure them of their joy! If Buddha had taken potassium bromides, worked only two hours a day, and drunk milk, that remarkable man would have left no more behind him than is left by a dog.

PESOTSKY

Just drink it, Andrei Vasilich!

KOVRIN

Why do you do this to me? Milk. Laziness. The two of you spying and measuring my every breath. Every swallow; every step. I was going mad, I had megalomania, but for all of it I was cheerful and high-spirited; I was interesting and original. Now I'm dull. I'm as dull and mediocre as the both of you.

PESOTSKY

I have said it and it's true; I welcome your insults. I am your target. Just do as the doctors have ordered.

KOVRIN

I had hallucinations, we agree. But in your eyes, tell me what was the harm?

PESOTSKY

I will tell you this, since you ask me. Nothing you're saying makes any sense or, as far as I can tell, has a speck of truth in it except for the point you make about being dull. You are dull. On that you are correct. You are dull. Kovrin is dull.

KOVRIN
Starting to drink his milk.
Then don't listen.

PESOTSKY
At last we agree.
He is ready to leave.
Tanya, I have accounting to do. Come to me when you can no longer stand to breathe the air he sickens.
Then to Kovrin.
As for you. I love you. Good-bye.
He goes, and Kovrin, watching, drinks glass after glass of milk.

TANYA
Your anger is killing him. I want you to understand, Kovrin. He grows old before my eyes. Not each day, not each week, but by the minute; by the second. Andryusha, why can't you be gentle with him?

KOVRIN
I don't want to.

TANYA
But why?

KOVRIN
Because I find him unpleasant, that's all.

TANYA
Pressing her temples.
I must go lie down, Kovrin. I'm sorry. I have a headache.

KOVRIN
Holding out the milk.
Drink some milk.

TANYA
This is torture; it's torture.
As she goes, he pursues her for a step or two after her.

KOVRIN
I agree. I am the monster, while you and your father are the little babies that I slaughter. You're the innocents that—
With Tanya gone, Kovrin sees Orlov, who has returned carrying a box.
Orlov! Good!
Hurrying over to grab the box.
Hurry up. There are two more. Faster now. Run.
Kovrin sets the box on the floor and strides back to grab a second box from Orlov, who has scurried off and come back, and off he goes again.
Stop wasting time. Hurry up.
He sets the second box down on the ground near the first.
We can work right here. Yes, yes.
His attention is seized by an item in the box and he bends and takes out several bound documents, which he contemplates and then shows to Orlov, who is back now with one last box.
My dissertation and certain articles I wrote when my illness filled me with abundant faith. I placed such hope in them.
Holding the manuscript open for Orlov.
Do you see?

ORLOV
So many words.

KOVRIN
Where's the wine? You didn't forget the wine.
Orlov plucks a wine bottle and glass from the last box.
Good. Pour it.
Pacing away, he takes a stack of paper from a box.
While I get on with the task at hand.
*With will and concentration, almost ritualistically, he tears
the document in half.*
I want you to help me. I was so proud.

ORLOV
What?

KOVRIN
Just do this!
Tearing more pages.

ORLOV
What should I do?

KOVRIN
Handing a stack to Orlov.
Do what I just did. Tear them to pieces.
Ripping more pages in half.

ORLOV
Clutching the papers, but hesitant, worried.
But this is your . . . words. It's the—

KOVRIN
Do you want me to beat you? Orlov! I will whip you like the monster that I am! This is what we are going to do!

He tears more, but still Orlov falters.
To all of it. Or do I grab a stick and—
    Orlov obeys, tearing a sheet.
Very good.
    Orlov continues ripping papers, and Kovrin lights the cigar.
Dust to dust to dust to dust. That's the way. Now you're getting
the hang of it.
    Sitting down with his cigar, he sips his wine.
Good man. Sturdy strong hands. You're born to it, Orlov.
    As Orlov continues.
What do you think? Burn the scraps? Or throw them into the air?
Fire? Or wind? Or both perhaps. Perhaps—
    Tanya comes rushing in.

TANYA
Kovrin, I smelled cigar smoke and—

KOVRIN
Come join us!

TANYA
What are you doing?
    Approaching in disbelief.
And wine! Kovrin! Orlov!
    Grabbing the bottle, thrusting it to Orlov.
Orlov, Orlov, Orlov! Get rid of this!

KOVRIN
Nooo! He's my assistant!
    He takes the bottle from Orlov, sets it on the table.

TANYA
Stop it.
    Now Kovrin begins tearing more papers, and she bends and
    picks fragments from the floor.
All your beautiful work! It's your work!

KOVRIN
Glancing at a page before he rips it up.
In every line pretension. The delusion of passion.
Tearing sheets, grabbing more.
You wanted to know my idea. This is it!
Tearing and throwing pieces to the floor.
Even the little punctuation marks are stupid. It's all—

TANYA
No more. Don't you dare harm another page! Orlov, stop. I demand it!
In the midst of tearing a sheet, Orlov freezes.

KOVRIN
Do as I say, Orlov, or I will tear you to pieces with them!

ORLOV
Yes, sir.
Starts ripping papers again.

KOVRIN
Waving a page at Tanya.
Every word. Every sentence. Megalomania.

TANYA
Kovrin, I beg you!

KOVRIN
Indicating a phrase.
Yes. Here! Obvious megalomania.
Tanya grabs Orlov, stopping him.

TANYA
Orlov! Bring my father here! Do it!
She shoves him in the way he must go and he hurries off.

KOVRIN
Reading and destroying.
My defects on display in gigantic typeface. In every phrase ineptitude. The ambitions of a child. Word after word of vanity and shame. All madness.
He dumps the box containing manuscripts and shredded paper onto the floor.

TANYA
Something's gone from you, it's gone, it's lost and it's never coming back.

KOVRIN
I know that.
He's woozy, sickened from the exertion, the wine, the cigar, and what he's done.
I have to stop, my head's spinning. A little wine and my heart's pounding. This cigar makes me sick.
He sinks to his knees as if he might vomit.

TANYA
Spite and hatred do not suit you. They make you ugly.
She grabs the cigar, puts it out in the wineglass.

KOVRIN
Do you think so?

TANYA
She moves to him, close.
But it will pass and Andryusha will come back. This is what I know. He will come back, and he will look at me the way he did— *you* will look at me the way you did that day you understood that we must marry. It will all come back.

KOVRIN
I must tell you something.

TANYA
What? Yes, please.

KOVRIN
You have it all wrong. It was not that moment, but earlier, crass manipulations that led to our so-called marriage.

TANYA
Retreating.
Don't insult our marriage. It is the dearest thing.

KOVRIN
They say that I am mad because I have delusions. Well, you, Tanya, are deluded also. Perhaps delusion is our common trait—I have my nonexistent monk, and you the preciousness of our marriage.

TANYA
You may no longer value our life together; I can't stop you. But I say it is a treasure. You stink of cigars and wine.
Pesotsky enters in a rush. Ready to take charge, he marches right up to Kovrin.

PESOTSKY
Wine and cigars! How could this happen? Inviting madness back!

KOVRIN
Yegor Semyonitch, I think you—

TANYA
Leave Father out of this!

KOVRIN
Tanya believes her marriage to me was born of romance and affection. I've been explaining to her the truth of how you begged me to marry her.

PESOTSKY
Stunned.
What?

KOVRIN
Aiming past Pesotsky at Tanya.
It was a matter of his business arrangements, Tanya. And if there
was love anywhere, it was his love of his beloved business.

PESOTSKY
Backing up.
What are you saying? What are you saying?
Rushing to Tanya.
Tanya! Ignore him!
*Pesotsky takes hold of Tanya; he puts himself between
Kovrin and Tanya and starts to move her to leave.*

KOVRIN
You came to me, you said, "What if she gets married?!" Tanya! He
was afraid that if you had children you would have no time for his
trees.
Tanya pulls free of her father, and Pesotsky turns to Kovrin.

PESOTSKY
You must not say these things, Kovrin.

KOVRIN
"Everything will go to ruin! Women are the scourge of God!"
Shouting past Pesotsky to Tanya.
Who do I sound like, Tanya? I think I represent him well!

TANYA
He would not say such things. Never!

KOVRIN
Of course he would. You know he would. You said yourself that
he has written out your thoughts! You are living in his dream!

TANYA
Tell me there is no truth in this, Father.

PESOTSKY
No, no, no. Not at all. None whatsoever.
*But she sees the truth in him, and he cannot keep her from
sinking to the floor.*

KOVRIN
Then drink milk! The both of you. Drink warm milk. Because you
are both deluded and altogether ignorant of the truth. Yegor Semyonitch, I was there. You know you stood before me and told me
I was the only man you would trust to marry Tanya. That if I married her, you would be happy.
To Tanya.
He prayed that I marry you, Tanya, because I alone could be
trusted to protect his farm, and so he prayed for some sort of romance between us.

PESOTSKY
Bending to her.
I said some of these things. But not in that way. Not to that pur-
pose.

KOVRIN
You would be so happy. You would be so happy!

PESOTSKY
Whirling to Kovrin.
Stop it! Stop it, stop it!
*As if to flee, Pesotsky moves upstage but he stops, and with
his back to Kovrin and Tanya, he begins to rock on his feet.
He bends as if in physical pain and groans the way he did
earlier, in that moment when he could not speak to Kovrin
about his desire for Tanya and Kovrin to marry. Pesotsky
bends and groans and rocks from foot to foot.*

TANYA
Father, don't do that. Please.

KOVRIN
Tanya, how else could such misery as ours be given the name of marriage?

TANYA
Father, you're frightening me.
    Staring at him.
What are you doing?

KOVRIN
He's trying to say something, but he cannot say it. Remember who you are, Yegor Semyonitch! You must be candid.
    Pesotsky groans, his feet banging up and down as his agony increases.

TANYA
Father, tell me what happened!

KOVRIN
No more so-called innermost thoughts. Let them come forth.
    Pesotsky makes a loud animal sound of suffering.

TANYA
It's true. You did it.
    Anguish overtaking her.
You've killed me.

PESOTSKY
Ahhhhhhhhhh! Ahhhhhhhhhhh!
    Wounded, he cries out.

TANYA
Father. Father.

114.

> *Pesotsky, making the lowing animal sounds of pain, stag-*
> *gers off.*

Father.

> *Then he is gone, and Tanya and Kovrin are alone with the*
> *wreckage. Music and changing lights.*

SCENE FOUR

> *After the preceding bedlam, there's a darkness, a stillness.*
> *And then a figure is revealed, a woman, VARVARA NIKO-*
> *LAEVNA, far upstage. She looks out.*

VARVARA NIKOLAEVNA

We do not desire frivolity. Be informed. My husband and I have
traveled here on the basis of recommendations that promised
order. They promised serenity and discretion.

> *The light widens to show that she speaks to a CON-*
> *CIERGE and a MAID in hotel uniforms.*

You must listen to me closely in order that you understand your
opportunity. Andrei Vasilich Kovrin, my husband, is a gifted,
highly regarded scholar and professor who merits your perfect devotion. It is an honor to attend him. If you have complaints, his
wife, bring them to me—bring your carping to me, Varvara Nikolaevna, his wife.

> *She looks them over.*

He was to have delivered his inaugural lecture at the university in Moscow on the second of December. The hallways
filled with excitement. The students and the faculty could talk
of little else once the announcement was made. But problems
developed and the lecture had to be canceled. Illness inter-
vened.

> *By now the lights have revealed a sense of space. A vast sky.*
> *The suggestion of a large window and a balcony. She*

watches a chair being brought in and placed by the BELL-
MAN, who she addresses.
I'm sorry to trouble you with the rearrangement of the furniture.
Nevertheless, we require it.
        And to them all.
We have come to your quiet, even pensive, establishment seeking rest for my husband. Rest in some scrupulous form, such as
one might grant a child. It is my hope that with your assistance,
we can restore him, bringing if not a complete rehabilitation, at
least a fair portion of health and vigor so that he may at last
make the great contribution of which he is capable. Now, I need
to know—have we been misled in the recommendations that
brought us here? For if we have, we will, in our unchecked dis-
appointment, depart.

CONCIERGE
No, madame. Trust that we are honored to assist you and your
husband in every way we can. You have our pledge.

VARVARA NIKOLAEVNA
I will need more than your pledge. I must have your deeds.

CONCIERGE
You may rely on us.

VARVARA NIKOLAEVNA
Thank you.
        Glancing off, as if she's heard something.

CONCIERGE
And the subject of his lectures, if I may ask?

VARVARA NIKOLAEVNA
I think he's coming now.

CONCIERGE
His subject matter, madame. Please.

VARVARA NIKOLAEVNA
Philosophy.

CONCIERGE
Oh. We are honored.
Kovrin enters, neatly dressed in a suit, walking slowly with a cane.
Good evening, sir.

HOTEL STAFF
Good evening, sir.
Good evening, sir.

VARVARA NIKOLAEVNA
I've been alerting the staff to our requirements.

KOVRIN
Fine. Good. Hello. Hello.

VARVARA NIKOLAEVNA
Well, then, thank you so much.
Gesturing that they leave.

CONCIERGE
If you should desire dinner, please notify us.

KOVRIN
I'm not hungry. I'm not hungry.

VARVARA NIKOLAEVNA
Well, then, goodnight.

CONCIERGE
Goodnight.

BELLMAN
Goodnight, sir. And madame.

VARVARA NIKOLAEVNA
Thank you. Goodnight.
When they are gone, she turns to him.
Your little stroll grew quite lengthy. I was worried you might over-exert yourself.

KOVRIN
No.

VARVARA NIKOLAEVNA
You didn't overdo it.

KOVRIN
No.

VARVARA NIKOLAEVNA
I must say, the train ride has left me exhausted. Though it was comfortable. You appear downcast, Kovrin.

KOVRIN
I'm sorry.

VARVARA NIKOLAEVNA
Don't be sorry. Just look around. Look where we are.
As she advances to the window.
We have arrived. Where the air smells of the sea.
Behind her, Kovrin settles down in the chair.
Shall I tell you a secret? While you were napping on the train, I reread your lecture, and I was struck again by its breathtaking, forceful erudition. I felt the presence of your mind. With each slight revision the complexity grows, and with it the clarity.

KOVRIN
Good.

VARVARA NIKOLAEVNA
If only you could move on to the next section. Why don't you reread it yourself? I think it would inspire you.

KOVRIN
I should, of course, but it's just . . . difficult at the moment.

VARVARA NIKOLAEVNA
I don't mean now. You're weary from the travel, but—

KOVRIN
I'm finding it all . . . difficult, Varvara.

VARVARA NIKOLAEVNA
Kovrin. Have there been symptoms again and you didn't tell me?

KOVRIN
No.

VARVARA NIKOLAEVNA
No signs of blood. You would never hide them from me.

KOVRIN
No.

VARVARA NIKOLAEVNA
Not a trace; you're sure.
As he nods.
It's a setback, of course. We can't pretend otherwise. We wouldn't want to. But I love recalling the excitement that overtook the university when your lecture was announced. In that memory I find a source of encouragement that makes me know that we must return; we must succeed. That we will succeed.
Kovrin has risen; he walks forward.

KOVRIN
The water—what color is the water?

VARVARA NIKOLAEVNA
The water? I can't say.

KOVRIN
Look how the moonlight mixes on the surface with the lights from the hotel. In some of the waves it seems almost a blue vitriol, do you see? Yet there are patches where it appears not water at all, but a kind of thickened moonlight.
As Kovrin gazes out the window, she joins him.

VARVARA NIKOLAEVNA
Well, no matter. For all of it, the mood is calm and lofty.

KOVRIN
But what is the color?

VARVARA NIKOLAEVNA
Kovrin, it's water; it's beautiful. Enjoy it.

KOVRIN
But I'd like to know. Is there no single word for such a color?

VARVARA NIKOLAEVNA
And so you say "blue vitriol," and I agree, but then you find it inadequate. You disagree with yourself.

KOVRIN
You're right. It's water. I'm sorry.

VARVARA NIKOLAEVNA
Of course it's discouraging the way your illness returned. But they don't know everything, these doctors. About you. About us.

KOVRIN
"Avoid worry," they told me. "Talk less." Such was their prescription. "But otherwise lead a regular life." Once it was "Don't work, drink milk." I was obedient in every way.

VARVARA NIKOLAEVNA

We have time. We have time. Your mother lived with her illness for many years. And soon it will be two months since there was the slightest blood in your throat.

Then voices and laughter rise to them.

Ahhh. Listen. The windows must be open below us. Apparently there's a party. Should I call down?

KOVRIN

No, that's not necessary.

VARVARA NIKOLAEVNA

Well, no harm then. You're sure you can sleep?

She starts toward the upstage bedroom door, expecting him to come with her.

KOVRIN

I'm not ready for bed, Varvara.

VARVARA NIKOLAEVNA

You must be, Kovrin.

KOVRIN

No. I'm tired, but not sleepy.

VARVARA NIKOLAEVNA

Well, I'm afraid I'm worn out.

Starting off.

Yes, let me confess, I need to lay down.

Faltering.

But . . . may I ask something?

KOVRIN

Of course.

VARVARA NIKOLAEVNA
You received a letter just before we left home for the train. It was from Tanya Pesotsky, wasn't it?

KOVRIN
You saw that.

VARVARA NIKOLAEVNA
I did. Forgive me, but of course I'm curious. Would you be willing to disclose the contents of what she wrote?

KOVRIN
I'm afraid we will never know the content, Varvara. I couldn't bring myself to open it at first, and it lay in my pocket for some time, but then the thought of it there, traveling with me, following me . . . well, it disturbed me. Even after two years. And I thought, no. I don't want it. I threw it away. I threw it into the trash while we were on the train.

VARVARA NIKOLAEVNA
You were not curious at all? I wonder what she could have thought to say to you.

KOVRIN
Sincerely, Varvara, in the depths of my soul I see my marriage to that woman as a cruel hoax. I cannot express how glad I am to have broken with her. Any memory whatsoever brings not curiosity but bitterness and enmity.

VARVARA NIKOLAEVNA
Now look. I ask you to rest and then I disturb you.
    Going.
Goodnight.

KOVRIN
When I last saw her she was a walking skeleton. Her large eyes stared out at me, but nothing else about her seemed alive.

VARVARA NIKOLAEVNA

Well.

KOVRIN

Yes.

VARVARA NIKOLAEVNA
As she goes.
Come in soon.

KOVRIN
I will. Goodnight.
> *Varvara Nikolaevna exits, and Kovrin takes the letter from his pocket. He looks out to the audience.*

I could not bear to share the truth with her.
> *He unfolds the letter and reads it aloud.*

Andrei Vasilich Kovrin, my father has just died. This I owe to you, as it was you who killed him. Our orchard is dying. Outsiders have taken it over already, and so the very thing poor father was so afraid of is happening. This, too, I owe to you. I hate you with all my soul and I hope that you will die soon. I want you to die. Oh, how this hurts! An excruciating pain burns inside my heart. I curse you. I took you for an extraordinary man, for a genius, I loved you, but you were insane, a madman, and for all the misery, for all—
> *Kovrin crumples the letter and drops it to the floor. From below come women's voices and laughter.*

KOVRIN
I hear them, and yet I feel there's not a single other living soul nearby.
> *Calling down.*

Hello! Do you hear me down there? Hello!
> *Varvara Nikolaevna comes out, sleepily, in a robe over a white dressing gown.*

VARVARA NIKOLAEVNA
Kovrin, what is it?

KOVRIN
Did I tell you that when I shredded my dissertation, a sudden wind came up?

VARVARA NIKOLAEVNA
Of course you told me. Please, Kovrin, sleep now, won't you?

KOVRIN
The scraps were thrown about, hurled in and out of windows and caught in trees! The pieces clung to flowers.

VARVARA NIKOLAEVNA
What's wrong?

KOVRIN
I don't know. I feel so full of regret and misery.

VARVARA NIKOLAEVNA
Don't suffer, my darling. Perhaps you should work. If you're too agitated to sleep—

KOVRIN
It's too late.

VARVARA NIKOLAEVNA
But why not work a little? When your nerves are scattered this way you know it sometimes soothes you.

KOVRIN
Yes. Perhaps. Bring my red briefcase. Bring it here.
She hurries off.
Alright, alright. I'll force myself. Yes. One thought. One thought.
Calling to her.

Inside there's a copybook. Bring just the copybook. I jotted down these notes for a small compilation which— No, no, bring the whole case.

VARVARA NIKOLAEVNA
Returning with the case.
What is the theme of your compilation?

KOVRIN
Well, it's— Why do you ask?

VARVARA NIKOLAEVNA
Because I hope you might produce a paper with a theme that could lead to recognition. The large success you deserve. So that the world might at last see your worth.

KOVRIN
So for you, then, the consummation of my effort is that I be honored by the world. That I receive the praise of my benumbed society. Yes, yes, that's my goal. Excitement in the halls. And for that I have given, I have sacrificed. Varvara Nikolaevna, think how much life extracts from us in exchange for the paltry gifts it can in fact bestow. Look at me. I have gained a university chair before the age of forty, and by doing this I have become a pedant who can render other people's thoughts as if they were my own. And in order to become this—parasite—I had to study for fifteen years. I had to endure deprivation and the misery of a mental breakdown—the ruin of a marriage, in which I committed offenses I would like to forget forever. And all this I did in order to become the mediocrity before you, whom I recognize and accept. Because, in my opinion, every person should be satisfied with what he is.

VARVARA NIKOLAEVNA
Kovrin, forgive me. I fear I've brought the opposite of what I intended.
Moving to the crumpled letter, she bends to pick it up.

KOVRIN
Sternly.
What are you doing?

VARVARA NIKOLAEVNA
Frozen above the letter, her arm outstretched toward it.
I thought I would just clean up this—

KOVRIN
No! Leave it. Just go to bed.

VARVARA NIKOLAEVNA
You're right.
Going.
You must have time alone. Of course. Goodnight.
Alone, he hears the party sounds from below.

KOVRIN
They have voices and I hear them, even though I feel that the earth has emptied of all worth, all . . . life, all value and—I am cursed.
Turning to the letter on the floor.
Poor sad Tanya, the hatred in her letter dooms me. I . . . am . . .
From below a violin begins to play and women's voices sing Braga's Serenade.
Ohhhh. Now. Now. What are we to do when it reminds us?
To the audience.
You remember it, don't you? You have to. I know you do, and don't you feel it? It must remind you! Do we dare remember? Do we dare recall what we felt, the sweetness that we knew?
The violin plays, the voices sing, as he looks to the window.
The sea grows dark and wild, the horizon a towering pillar, as if that whirlwind that brought such ruin to my life will soon pour into this room once more.

THE BLACK MONK
Oh, Kovrin, Kovrin.
The Black Monk appears.

KOVRIN
Yes.

THE BLACK MONK
Reproachful, yet tender.
Why didn't you believe me? If only you had believed me then, that
you are a great man, you would not have wasted these past years
so sadly.

KOVRIN
I know. I had no choice, I thought.

THE BLACK MONK
But weren't we privileged to share so many lofty, fascinating
conversations?

KOVRIN
They were splendid. And invigorating. Each a lavish adventure.

THE BLACK MONK
I enjoyed them so much. Can you recall one for me? Please remind
me of one. Recall some wondrous phrase of all that we said.

KOVRIN
I can't. Once everything was fixed in my mind, but now I'm not—I
don't quite— And yet there was one—there was one—
He stops.

THE BLACK MONK
Yes. What did we say?

KOVRIN
We said— We said—

THE BLACK MONK
Tell me all of it!

KOVRIN
Am I not—am I not still, as I believed then—
Kovrin coughs, and there is blood, a little on his hands, and handkerchief, a small amount showing on his lips. He raises the handkerchief toward The Black Monk.
Look . . . , look . . .

THE BLACK MONK
You're ill. You're hurt. You must have help.
Kovrin coughs, struggles to breathe.
Who sleeps beyond the wall, Kovrin? Someone sleeps beyond that wall.

KOVRIN
Looking to the wall.
Varvara Nikolaevna.
He coughs, blood spills out of his mouth onto his chest, and he stares at his hands, his shirt cuffs and handkerchief red with blood.

THE BLACK MONK
You must have help, Kovrin.

KOVRIN
Yes.

THE BLACK MONK
You must call for help.

KOVRIN
Yes. She will help me.

THE BLACK MONK
Call now. Now.

KOVRIN
Tanya . . . !

THE BLACK MONK
Who is it that you call?

KOVRIN
He struggles for breath.
Tanya . . . !

THE BLACK MONK
Is it Tanya that you call?

KOVRIN
Yes! I want to call to Tanya.

THE BLACK MONK
All right.

KOVRIN
I want to call to Tanya. And to the garden. I want to call to the big garden with its splendid flowers wet with dew.

THE BLACK MONK
Wonderful! Yes! And to the pine trees with their shaggy roots!

KOVRIN
I want to call to the rye field! And to the poor ducks that I frightened that day.

THE BLACK MONK
Yes, yes.

KOVRIN
I want to call to my books! To my studies.

THE BLACK MONK
Oh, you must! Now! Yes! Call to your books—to your marvelous studies! Call to your youth. To courage, and joy.

KOVRIN
I want to call to my life, which has been so beautiful!

THE BLACK MONK
I want that, too. Call for us both. Call now!

KOVRIN
Oh, life! Oh, life!
He tries for more but manages only breath. From below, the violin plays, and the serenade is sung, as wind comes up and Kovrin sinks to his knees. The Black Monk looks on.

THE BLACK MONK
Kovrin, good friend, my delight, how I love you. How great you are.

VARVARA NIKOLAEVNA
Calling from offstage.
What is this noise? Such a wind?
Slowly Kovrin sinks from his knees to his side.

THE BLACK MONK
But listen to me now! In these last seconds hear my last words for you. Please, Kovrin! Understand! You are dying only because your

weak human body can no longer serve as a vessel to contain your great genius.

> *Kovrin, lying on his back with his head downstage, manages a breath as Varvara Nikolaevna enters in her night clothes, a white, seeming phantom.*

VARVARA NIKOLAEVNA
Seeing Kovrin.
Kovrin, it's going to storm. Why are you—
> *She freezes.*

THE BLACK MONK
You must believe that you are, as you once knew, a man touched by God and greatness.

KOVRIN
But . . . something happened. What happened?

THE BLACK MONK
Oh, Kovrin, don't you know? You forgot me and all that I said.

KOVRIN
I forgot.
> *Simply, happily, realizing.*
I forgot.

THE BLACK MONK
But now . . . you remember.
> *The Black Monk stands looking down at Kovrin.*

VARVARA NIKOLAEVNA
She approaches, fearfully.
Oh, no. Oh, Kovrin. Little Kovrin.
> *Sinking to him, kneeling. With Kovrin's back to the audience, it appears he looks up past her at The Black Monk. Only she can see his face.*

What? What? Look at you. Your face so full of bliss. Now? Now?

> *From below, the violin and singing grow, while Varvara kneels and The Black Monk goes. Unable to see Kovrin's face, we have only her words.*

Oh, Kovrin. At what do you smile? At what do you smile?

MUSIC
BLACKOUT

Praise for *THE DOG PROBLEM*

"A dark comedy . . . only tenuously tethered to realism . . . it has the kind of sneaky impact that may catch up with you—as it did me—long after you leave the theater."

—BRUCE WEBER, *THE NEW YORK TIMES*

"Do you know when to grovel and when not to gloat? The finer points of such behavior are a lesson that is central . . . in David Rabe's dark comedy. . . . For those who equate Rabe with the hard edge of his Vietnam plays . . . *The Dog Problem* will come as something of a surprise. It's wickedly funny."

—LES GUTMAN, *CURTAINUP*

"The nature of friendship, the importance of loyalty, and the quest for safety in a cosmic sense . . . transform into flights of metaphor . . . a believable group portrait of men in crisis dogged by their too-human flaws."

—IRIS FANGER, *THE BOSTON PHOENIX*

Trouble starts when Teresa tells her brother, Joey, that this guy Ray did something to her with his dog in bed. Nobody seems to know exactly what happened, but they do know that somebody's got to pay. So what is *The Dog Problem*? It starts with being born into a world where the wrong thing said to the wrong person ignites a chain reaction of misplaced passions and galloping sentences that race to a deadly conclusion. The playful title is revealed to be a wry pun on the Cartesian mind/body problem, as Uncle Mal, the aging mobster, must face his turn to be the dog in this darkly funny play about men, women, sex, betrayal, and ghosts.

Vastly different in their aesthetic, these two highly praised plays embody the celebrated hallmarks of David Rabe's writing and art: unflinchingly honest and perceptive themes, starkly luminous dialogue, and the unsettling humor which have made him an icon of the American theater for more than forty years.

 **DAVID RABE** is the author of many widely performed plays, including *The Basic Training of Pavlo Hummel, Sticks and Bones, In the Boom Boom Room, Streamers, Hurlyburly,* and *The Dog Problem.* Four of his plays have been nominated for the Tony Award, including a win for Best Play. He is the recipient of an Obie Award, the American Academy of Arts and Letters Award, Drama Desk Award, and the New York Drama Critics Circle Award, among others. His numerous screenwriting credits include *I'm Dancing As Fast As I Can, Casualties of War, Hurlyburly,* and *The Firm.*

Rabe is the critically acclaimed author of the novels *Dinosaurs on the Roof* and *Recital of the Dog,* and a collection of short stories, *A Primitive Heart.* Born in Dubuque, Iowa, Rabe lives with his family in northwest Connecticut.

ALSO BY DAVID RABE

Plays
Cosmologies
A Question of Mercy
(based on the diary of Richard Selzer)
Those the River Keeps
Hurlyburly
Goose and Tomtom
In the Boom Boom Room

The Vietnam Plays
Streamers
The Orphan
Sticks and Bones
The Basic Training of Pavlo Hummel

Fiction
Dinosaurs on the Roof
A Primitive Heart
Recital of the Dog

Children's Books
Mr. Wellington

the dog problem

David Rabe

SIMON & SCHUSTER PAPERBACKS
New York   London   Toronto   Sydney

Simon & Schuster
1230 Avenue of the Americas
New York, NY 10020

First Simon & Schuster trade paperback edition July 2009

SIMON & SCHUSTER and colophon are registered trademarks
of Simon & Schuster, Inc.

For information about special discounts for bulk purchases,
please contact Simon & Schuster Special Sales at 1-866-506-1949
or business@simonandschuster.com.

The Simon & Schuster Speakers Bureau can bring authors to your live event.
For more information or to book an event contact the Simon & Schuster
Speakers Bureau at 1-866-248-3049 or visit our website at
www.simonspeakers.com.

Designed by Jaime Putorti

Manufactured in the United States of America

10   9   8   7   6   5   4   3   2   1

Library of Congress Cataloging-in-Publication Data

Rabe, David.
   The black monk ; and, The dog problem : two plays / David Rabe.
      p. cm.
   I. Rabe, David. Dog problem. II. Title.
PS3568.A23B53 2009
812'.54—dc22

                                                                    2009017588

ISBN 978-1-4391-4188-5 (trade pbk.)

FOR THE DOGS

MICKEY

MIDNIGHT

BLUEBERRY

FLASH

RUBY

TRICKS

SAZ

TIZJA

PHOEBE

First Presented in Workshop by
Williamstown Theatre Festival

Michael Ritchie, Producer

World Premiere Production
The Long Wharf Theatre

Douglas Hughes   Michael Ross
Artistic Director   Managing Director

Originally Produced in New York
by
Evangeline Morphos

For the Long Wharf Theatre, Doug Hughes production, the director was Scott Ellis; the set design was by Alan Moyer; lighting design was by Brian Nason; costume design was by Michael Krass; the sound design was by Eileen Tague.

THE CAST

Ronnie	Joe Pacheco
Ray	Larry Clarke
Joey	David Wike
Uncle Malvolio	Victor Argo
Tommy Stones	Tony Cucci
Teresa	Andrea Gabriel
The Priest	Michael Kell
The Dog	Ed

For the New York, Evangeline Morphos production, the director was Scott Ellis; the set design was by Alan Moyer; lighting design was by Brian Nason; costume design was by Michael Krass; the sound design was by Eileen Tague.

THE CAST

Ronnie	Joe Pacheco
Ray	Larry Clarke
Joey	David Wike
Uncle Malvolio	Victor Argo
Tommy Stones	Tony Cucci
Teresa	Andrea Gabriel
The Priest	Robert Bella
The Dog	Buddy

This edition incorporates a number of changes and additions.

CAST

RONNIE

RAY

JOEY

UNCLE MALVOLIO

TOMMY STONES

DOG

TERESA

PRIEST

Between Acts I and II
there is a time passage of
six months.

ACT ONE

The set is urban: brick walls, odd colors, maybe red, green across the back. Somebody painted over the brick. Stage right juts out with a bulky presence. Stage left is dominated by a large dumpster, nearby a pair of battered garbage cans. Slightly upstage and right of center, a lamppost stands, rising out of sight. Tattered posters and handbills are pasted to the sides and base of the lamppost. A door in the stage right wall has posters, a sign that reads Keep Out: Restricted Area. The floor pattern suggests concrete, a sidewalk, a street. Framing the front of the stage is a large metallic grid that runs up both stage left and right and is joined across the top by a horizontal section. There is a small playing area in front of the grid on both stage left and right. There are entranceways right and left that are blocked from sight by the grid, enabling characters to pop on from downstage left and right. There are also upstage right and left entrances, the up left bringing people in almost up center as they come around the wall fronted by the dumpster.

MUSIC. LIGHTS UP. RONNIE stands at the lamppost, smoking a cigarette, holding a paper bag containing two coffees. He bounces from one foot to the other. Then RAY enters from up left and hurries down to Ronnie.

RONNIE
Hey, Ray.

RAY
Yeah, yeah.

RONNIE
I been waitin'.

RAY
I know, I'm late. Listen, Ronnie.

RONNIE
You want some coffee?

RAY
No! Listen!
Facing Ronnie; this is important.

RONNIE
Yeah.

RAY
I'm gonna go.

RONNIE
What?

RAY
I gotta go.
He starts to go.

RONNIE
What are you talking about? You just got here.

RAY
My teeth hurt.

RONNIE
Your teeth hurt? Whatsamatter with them?

RAY
What do I know? They hurt. I wanna go brush them.

RONNIE
You should see a dentist, you know.

RAY
I know. I'm gonna go brush 'em.

RONNIE
Moving to halt Ray.
Did it just come out of the blue, or what? No warning signs?
Whata bitch. Here, have some coffee.
Offering one of the coffees.

RAY
I don't wanna drink coffee my teeth hurt, for crissake, whatsamatter with you? They're sensitive, you know.
Starting to go again.
I'm gonna go. Where you gonna be later?

RONNIE
Pointing out front.
Look at that!

RAY
What? Who?
He stops, looks.

RONNIE
Over there! Over there!

RAY
Those guys?
Moving downstage to look more closely out front.

RONNIE
You know that one?

RAY
Who?

RONNIE

That one! The one he just went around the corner. He was wearing the plaid thing, the red baseball cap.

RAY

No, I don't know him.

RONNIE

Sure you do! Yes, you do.

RAY

Ronnie, I don't. The guy in the red hat?

RONNIE

The plaid thing.

RAY

I don't know him.

RONNIE

I thought you did.

RAY

I don't.

RONNIE

Because I thought he looked like somebody I thought I saw you with.

RAY

Yeah? Where?

RONNIE

I don't remember.

RAY

Do you know why you don't remember? Because it didn't happen.

RONNIE

Are you sure?

RAY

So where was it you saw me and this guy together?

RONNIE

I don't remember.

RAY

Because you're not remembering! You're imagining, and you got it confused. You are mentally confused.

RONNIE

Not the way I look at it.

RAY

You got your memory thing mixed up with your imagination thing. You see him, and for whatever unknown reason, you put me with him! The fact I never met this guy in my life is of no concern to you. Then you mislabel this fucking mess memory and from that day forward, you're all mixed up on this score. All right? I'm gonna go.

Starting upstage once more.

RONNIE

Pointing out at a different angle.

Here comes somebody!

RAY

Whirling, a little irritated.

There's always somebody comin'! We're outside, this is a public venue.

> RONNIE

No, no, look at him.

> RAY

Who? That guy?

> RONNIE

Yeah.

> RAY
> *Returning to get a better look.*

I don't know him.

> RONNIE

Don't he look familiar?

> RAY

You gonna start it again? I hope not.

> RONNIE

No. I'm just sayin', he looks familiar.

> RAY

SO MAYBE YOU KNOW HIM!

> RONNIE

No.

> RAY

Fucking everybody starts to look familiar, you know.
> *As Ray faces Ronnie, JOEY enters from an upstage angle*
> *behind Ray. Ray, focused on Ronnie, or glancing off at the*
> *guys Ronnie was talking about, does not see Joey.*

We're all eatin' the same crap now, the same donuts and burgers and fries, you know. Gimme a cup of coffee. That's all we say. Gimme a Big Mac and a McNuggets. That's all any of us know how to say. Next thing, we all look alike.

> *Joey is now standing behind Ray, who senses him, turns.*

What? What?

JOEY

Do you know who I am?

RAY

What?

JOEY

Do you know who I am?
> *Then to Ronnie.*

Whatsamatter, you didn't tell him?

RAY
> *To Ronnie.*

Who is this guy? You know this guy?

JOEY

So you don't know me.

RAY

No.

JOEY

Do you want to know who you do know if you don't know me?
You know my sister. That's who you know.

RAY

I don't think so.
> *Ray is facing Joey now. Ronnie drifts off behind Ray.*

JOEY

I do. I think so.

RAY

I don't.

> **JOEY**

How do you know you don't know her? You could know her.

> **RAY**

Except I would never go out with any broad she shared a gene pool with a douche bag he looked like you! Would I, Ronnie?
> *As he turns back to share his joke with Ronnie, Joey whacks*
> *Ray in the stomach and Ray drops to his knees.*

Owwwww! What the fuck?

> **JOEY**
> *Pulling a large automatic handgun, which he makes sure*
> *Ray sees.*

Get up! Who said you went out with her?
> *He grabs Ray to force him to his feet.*

> **RAY**

You did! You come up to me, you says . . .
> *Ray struggles upright, as Joey hides the gun against*
> *his own body, under his arm. Ronnie retreats to the*
> *dumpster, getting the mass of it between himself and the*
> *action.*

> **JOEY**

I says, you knew her! That's all I says!

> **RAY**

Yeah?

> **JOEY**

Remember?

> **RAY**

No.

JOEY

She says you made her do something she didn't like. How about that? Do you remember that?

RAY

She liked it.

> *Ray backs up a few steps, stealing glances at Ronnie, but fearful of looking away from Joey and the gun.*

JOEY

You admit it, then.

RAY

I don't even know what we're talking about.

JOEY

MY SISTER! SHE SAYS—

RAY

The women I am with are very happy with how I treat them. They leave me happy!

> *Backing up, he clatters into the garbage cans, slams against the dumpster, where he is trapped.*

I'm happy, they're happy. We're all happy.

JOEY

I would not soil my lips with the garbage necessary to describe what you did to her.

RAY

What?

JOEY

I just said I would not soil my lips. That's what I said. Or do you wanna hear me talk about it? Is that what you like? You phone people up and make 'em talk dirty?

RAY

No.

JOEY

So what do you like?

RAY

You gotta give me a hint here, about who we're in fact talking about, because—

JOEY

Teresa.

RAY

I didn't know she was your sister.

JOEY

Is that my fault! Am I to ignore the twenty-two years she and I have shared, the Christmases, the birthdays, breakfasts, our socks in the same drawer and I am just supposed to wipe it out because you didn't know about it! UNLESS THEY ARE AN ONLY CHILD EVERYBODY'S GOT A SISTER, EVERYBODY'S GOT A BROTHER!

RAY

I thought she was one!

JOEY

She didn't have a brother!

RAY

Right. She didn't have a brother—she didn't have a sister.

JOEY

She was an only child.

RAY
That's what I thought.
> *Whirling to Ronnie, who is crouching behind the far end of
> the dumpster.*
Who is this guy?

JOEY
So you would take advantage of her?! Like she was a fucking orphan! You could abuse her! She had nobody in the world!

RAY
She seemed to be enjoying herself, I swear it—I thought I was doin' her a favor.

JOEY
But to involve her with a dog.

RAY
What?

JOEY
To involve her with an animal. That's perverted!

RAY
Whata you mean?

JOEY
That's against God and nature!

RONNIE
> *Peeking over the dumpster.*
Ray, you did it with a dog?

RAY
No, no, no.

JOEY

YOU CALLIN' HER A LIAR? SO YOU THINK YOU CAN BESMIRCH TERESA NOW ON TOP OF EVERYTHING ELSE.

Waving the gun, aiming it.

RAY

He watched! He didn't do nothin'!

RONNIE

Who?

RAY

What?

JOEY

Who watched?

RAY

The dog.

JOEY

That's sick.

Hiding the gun against his body.

RONNIE

I didn't know this part.

RAY

He lives there. He was in the room. The dog lives in the room. That's all. It's his room, too. He's my dog. I'm his person. We share the fucking room. He slept half the time.

JOEY

That's not what she said.

RAY
What'd she say?

JOEY
She said what you did to her and she told me, she said I should
shoot your eyes out and then I should take the keys out of your
pocket, and I should take out your billfold and read the address
and when I had the address, I should go to your apartment and
put three in your dog's head!
> *With the gun Joey forces Ray down on his knees, facing out
> and bent over one of the garbage cans.*

RAY
Listen to me.

JOEY
You should say your prayers.
> *Joey cocks the gun, and Ronnie ducks behind the dumpster
> as Joey jams the gun against the back of Ray's head.*

RAY
The dog had nothin' to do with it.

RONNIE
This is your dog, Ray! We're talking about—

RAY
OF COURSE IT'S MY DOG! THAT'S WHAT WE'RE TALK-
ING ABOUT!

JOEY
Where is he?

RAY
Who? The dog?

JOEY
WHERE IS HE?

RAY
Just answer me one thing? I got one question. In all those years—

JOEY
WHAT! WHAT! WHAT!

RAY
In all those years—

JOEY
WHAT'S YOUR FUCKING QUESTION?
Miming shooting him.
BANG! BANG! BANG!

RAY
Kneeling, kind of praying.
In all those years, right? That's what I'm talking about, and there
were the breakfasts and the socks in the drawers, and the Christ-
mas ornaments, and you know, whatever— Are you trying to tell
me that she never—in all those years, she never tol' you something
it wasn't true. I'm not saying she lied, but she seemed to me like a
very high-strung girl—she could get things confused, she could ex-
aggerate, that's what I'm saying—did that never happen?

JOEY
Whata you care?

RAY
Whata you mean? Isn't it obvious why I would be interested in
she's high-strung—she exaggerates—she gets the facts confused?

RONNIE
Reaching out over the top of the dumpster.

Hey, Joey, everybody gets the facts confused. Maybe that is what happened.

RAY

That's my point! Who can keep anything straight? That's what we're talking about—that's why we're here, talking.

JOEY

So what's your point?

RAY

That her facts, God help her, the poor little thing—her facts are not THE facts—that she is exaggerating, because we did it straight up in the regular you-look-em-in-the-eye position, and that's all that happened. I swear it on my mother's grave.
Joey wavers, pulls back a little.
She's said things in the past, you couldn't take her word for it. You already admitted it! This is another one of those times. Have I ever lied to you?

JOEY

I don't even know you.
Backing up a step.

RAY

That's what I'm saying. So where's our problem?

JOEY

Enraged again, ready to get back at Ray.
The dog, you fucking moron. The dog is our problem. I should shoot you right now.

RAY

Maybe she just wanted some attention from you. Did you ever think of that? Do you give her enough attention?

JOEY
I give her a lot of attention.

RAY
But is it enough? Is it enough?

JOEY
How do I know? I don't know. I'm a busy guy.
Turning away.

RAY
So maybe this is a plea from her of some kind. Maybe this is a plea on her part.

JOEY
Fuck you!

RAY
I'm not saying you're wrong. I'm just saying they get completely deranged on things like this—they will do anything to get your attention.

JOEY
I still think I should fucking clip you.

RAY
What for?

JOEY
I just think I should.

RAY
And go to jail?

JOEY
Why would I go to jail? Who says I'd go to jail?

RAY
They'd catch you.

JOEY
Who says?

RAY
I just think they'd catch you. Whata you think, Ronnie?

RONNIE
Still crouched behind the dumpster.
What?

JOEY
What do you think? Would they catch me?

RAY
I mean, they catch everybody sooner or later.

JOEY
WHAT ARE YOU TALKING ABOUT? WHAT THE FUCK
ARE YOU TALKING ABOUT? They don't catch everybody!
They do not catch EVERYBODY.

RAY
They catch a lot of people.

JOEY
Confused, frustrated.
Look! I'm sick of this!

RAY
All right.

JOEY
I'm sick of it, you hear me!

RAY

Sure, sure.

JOEY

They wouldn't catch me! She comes to me, you know! She's beggin'! What am I supposed to do?

RAY

Look, you did the right thing! But maybe enough is enough.

JOEY

I'm sick a this.

RAY

That's what I'm saying. Why should this go any further? I'm sick a this, too.

JOEY

I got better things to do.

RAY

We all got better things to do.

JOEY

I'm gonna go rent a movie.

RAY

That's right. Show yourself a good time.

JOEY

Shut up!
    Then to Ronnie.
As far as you and me, Ronnie, we're even.

RONNIE

What movie?

JOEY

I don't know what movie. I'll look over the shelves. Something
with explosions. And a guy like me. He's got a heart of gold.
Nobody knows what makes him tick. He walks the streets.

He steps to go, then faces Ray one last time.

Just because I have left you off the hook in this case, don't think
you know what it means about me because you don't!

*Joey stalks off up right. Ronnie emerges from behind the
dumpster, looking after Joey, as Ray takes a deep breath,
leans against the lamppost.*

RONNIE

What an asshole!

RAY

You think so?

RONNIE

Yeah.

RAY

You think he's an asshole?

RONNIE

Yeah. Don't you?

RAY

Yeah, well, sure. But he doesn't say to me, you know, "we're even."
He doesn't say that. What's he mean, he says, "we're even?"

RONNIE

You mean to me?

RAY

He said it to you, Ronnie.

RONNIE
I owed him money.

RAY
Oh. You owed him money.
Turning, pacing away.
Ronnie, Ronnie, Ronnie.

RONNIE
What?

RAY
This is sad. This is terrible. This is sad, Ronnie.

RONNIE
I know. You're right.

RAY
You owed him money.

RONNIE
Yeah.

RAY
I see. I get it.

RONNIE
Guiltily, sitting on one of the trash cans.
Yeah.

RAY
A lot of money.

RONNIE
It was a lot of money.

RAY
So he says you gotta distract me to this corner and keep me here.

RONNIE
He says he wants to scare you.

RAY
Fuck him, he's an asshole, he couldn't scare a little girl.
Charging back to confront Ronnie.
But that's it, huh? That's what you were doin' with all that stuff before about that guy and did I know him?

RONNIE
What guy?
Ray grabs Ronnie and pushes him to the spot they stood on earlier, looking out at the various guys.

RAY
THE GUY IN THE RED HAT! THAT PLAID THING! THAT GUY!

RONNIE
I didn't think I had a choice.

RAY
Of course you had a choice. You had a choice.

RONNIE
I didn't think I did. It didn't seem like I did. To me. I mean, to me, as far as I could see, I didn't think I did.

RAY
Whata you think now?

RONNIE
Are you mad at me?

RAY

As far as my feelings go, I ain't made up my mind yet. I mean, I gotta say to myself, every time I'm standing around on the corner with you for the rest of my life, I gotta say to myself, can I trust this guy—can I trust him—do I have to watch out for somethin'?

RONNIE

No. You do not. I'm tellin' you, Ray, you—

RAY

You're tellin' me.

RONNIE

That's right.

RAY

But you're a liar in my eyes. You have proven yourself a liar! What about that?

RONNIE

You're right.

RAY

I know I'm right.

RONNIE

He's connected, that guy.

RAY

What guy?

RONNIE

That guy! The guy he come up here, he—

RAY

That guy? He's connected?

RONNIE

Yes. He is. Indirectly. I know it for a fact.

RAY

You know it for a fact indirectly, or he is connected indirectly.

RONNIE

I'm sorry. I'm sorry about what's happened between us, Ray, that's all I can say. What more can I say?

> *Having paced to the dumpster, Ray slams it with the palm of his hand.*

RAY

His sister had big tits, you know. That's what happened. She had these boomers and the dog went nuts.

RONNIE

And then what?

> *Leaning on the dumpster, as if on a bar.*

I wish I'd been there.

RAY

I wish you hadda, too, because then you coulda been on Teresa's fucking hit list, too, and her jerkoff brother could not have ever come to you like he did, to use you against me, like some miserable squirrel, he throws you a nut, you lose your dignity, you lose your soul over some fucking acorn. We coulda avoided this whole thing.

RONNIE

How's your tooth?

RAY

I feel you have betrayed me.

RONNIE

I have betrayed you.

RAY

My tooth hurts. I don't know how you could do this to me.

RONNIE

So it's over then, our friendship?

RAY

I don't think—if the truth be told—it was ever a friendship, actually ever, anyway.
        Starting to walk away.
That's what I think.

RONNIE

No? What was it?

RAY

I don't know. It was something new—you know, modern.
        He stops, steps back.
A very modern relationship. We were like, you know, a couple of
guys in a beer commercial.

RONNIE

Like those frogs.

RAY

No!

RONNIE

Sure.

RAY

No! Not the frogs! The frogs have something real. Something ad-
mirable. We were more like a couple of male models—these male
models pretending something. Posing. We were in an advertise-
ment so that we were involved in nothing but an exchange of
goods. Commodities. It was narcissism, you know. Nothing more!
        Ray goes.

RONNIE
Looking off after Ray.
Your dog gets you into trouble, Ray, how is that my fault? I don't think so.
He turns, looking skyward as he crosses to throw the coffee into the dumpster.
I always thought there was something funny about that dog.
His cell phone rings with its distinct ring. Throughout, each character's cell phone has an individual ring. Now Ronnie plucks his cell phone from his pocket.
Yeah?
Joey appears on the downstage right corner, backed by brick wall, his cell phone to his ear.

JOEY
Ronnie, it's me. Are you alone?

RONNIE
Who is this?

JOEY
Where are you?

RONNIE
Who is this? Joey, is that you?

JOEY
Are you alone, or not, Ronnie? Tell me the fucking truth.

RONNIE
Yeah, yeah. I'm alone.

JOEY
What about your buddy, the smart-ass?

RONNIE
No, no, I'm alone.

JOEY
I can't let this go. Where are you?

RONNIE
I'm where I was. On the corner. Where are you?

JOEY
I'm a few blocks away. That's as far as I got.

RONNIE
You can't let what go?

JOEY
I'm a few blocks away on the corner. I come to an abrupt halt. I'm walking along, I'm trying to let it go, all of a sudden, all of a fucking sudden, Ronnie, I can't take another step. I'm standing here.

RONNIE
Where?

JOEY
On the corner.

RONNIE
What corner?

JOEY
Looking.
I'm at Crosby and Houston. Almost to Lafayette. Listen. I'm going to start walking toward you. You start walking toward me.

RONNIE
You can't let what go, Joey?

JOEY

Start walking. You walk north. You're on the corner of Bowery and Grand where I left you?

RONNIE

Yeah.

JOEY

You start walking west on Broome—that's heading toward Elizabeth. I'll go east on Prince and then I'll turn south when I get to Mulberry—you go north.

RONNIE

What?

JOEY

You go north on Mott when you get there.

RONNIE

What's going on?

JOEY

I wanna meet you. ARE YOU WALKING?!

RONNIE

Yeah. Sure.
Joey steps in front of the stage right grid, while Ronnie moves down to stand in front of the stage left grid.
I'm walking. We're going to meet going north and south on Mott.

JOEY

That's right. That's fucking right.
Separated by the width of the stage, each in his own pool of light, a faint traffic sound beneath them, they face front, talk on their cell phones and pantomime walking.
Where are you now?

RONNIE

I'm about halfway to Kenmare—where are you?

JOEY

Don't worry about it. That douche bag. Where does he get off?

RONNIE

Who?

JOEY

What are you asking me? What the hell are you asking me?

RONNIE

You says somebody's a douche bag? I wanna know who!

JOEY

Don't make me lose my fucking patience with you, Ronnie! Is that what you're trying to do?

RONNIE

No.

JOEY

Then what are you doing you say "WHO?" to me after what I just been through? What are you, a fucking owl?

RONNIE

No.

JOEY

So what are you? What the fuck are you, Ronnie?

RONNIE

I'm a squirrel, looking for acorns.

JOEY

So where are you now?

RONNIE
You mean on the street? Where am I on the street?

JOEY
No. In the great inner workings of everything! Of course on the street, you asshole!

RONNIE
I'm gettin' a little tired of all this abuse, Joey.

JOEY
Who cares?

RONNIE
I'm almost to the corner. I don't know why you can't let it go.

JOEY
He didn't grovel.

RONNIE
Who? Ray? He groveled! What are you saying? Of course he grov-eled.

JOEY
That wasn't groveling.

RONNIE
I thought it was.

JOEY
You think that was groveling? Where are you?

RONNIE
I'm turning the corner.
Stepping away from the grid, he stands down left.

JOEY
I don't see you.
Stepping away from the grid, he stands down right.

RONNIE
Well I'm here.
*Still separated by the width of the stage and standing in
pools of light, they look this way and that way, searching
for each other.*

JOEY
I don't see you.

RONNIE
I don't see you either.

JOEY
I can't let it go. It's eatin' at me, Ronnie. It's eatin' at me. This guy's
a friend of yours, right?

RONNIE
Not anymore. He thinks I betrayed him. I mean, I did betray him.

JOEY
Everybody betrays everybody, Ronnie.

RONNIE
I know.

JOEY
You know that. Get used to it. Grow up. You both should
grow up.
He discovers Ronnie.
There you are!

RONNIE
What?

JOEY
I see you.
 Waving.

RONNIE
Where?
 Looking around.

JOEY
You're right there in front of the cigar store.

RONNIE
 Looking up.
Right. I am. I don't see you though.

JOEY
I'm across the street.

RONNIE
 Turning, focusing on Joey.
Oh, yeah. There you are.

JOEY
You see me now?

RONNIE
 Waving.
Yeah, sure. You're right there.
 They each stride toward the other, meeting down center,
 where they snap their cell phones shut, and the lights widen
 to hold them both.
He groveled, Joey.

JOEY
I'm going to call my uncle.

RONNIE
He groveled, I swear it to you. Don't call your uncle.

JOEY
I feel I have to.
Dialing.

RONNIE
No, no. Whata you mean.

JOEY
I think it's important you should know—that's what I wanted to tell you. I'm calling my Uncle Malvolio.

RONNIE
You don't have to do that? Why?

JOEY
This guy humiliates me in front of you. The two of you are gloating—you think I don't see it?

RONNIE
What are you talking about? Nobody was gloating. He was groveling. Ray was groveling!
Dialing his own cell phone.
I don't know what more he could have done to grovel more, but I'm sure he will once we let him know it's required. And I sure as hell was not gloating, Joey, I was not—

JOEY
Waving, he shuts Ronnie up, then speaks into the phone.
Hey, hey, Tommy, excuse me, but this is Joey. Could I speak to my uncle, please? Sure. No, no, I don't mind, I'm happy to hold.

What? No, no, I'm fine, Tommy. How are you? How's the family?
Good. Good.

> *Pause.*

Yeah, I'll be right here.

> *To Ronnie.*

He's gettin' him.

RONNIE

> *Closing his phone, despairingly.*

Listen, Joey—you gotta understand, I don't know what I was
doing. But I do know what I was NOT doing, and as God is my
witness, I was NOT gloating . . . and Ray—I swear to you—he was
groveling. That was *groveling,* he—

JOEY

You think I don't know the difference between *gloating* and *groveling*? I saw the two of you. I was there.

RONNIE

Of course.

JOEY

Don't forget that. Did you forget that?

RONNIE

No, no. But if you think about it for just a second, Joey, why
would I gloat? What do I got to gloat about?

JOEY

You don't know why you were doing such a jerkoff thing, that's
your problem. I can't handle everything. You go around gloating
without knowing why. That's not something I can help you with.
But from where I stand, I know what I saw, and I cannot, I cannot
let it go, so if I were you—

> *Into phone.*

Yes, Uncle Mal, hello. Thank you for taking my call. I appreciate
it. I'm sorry to bother you on such a trivial problem, but— What?

Oh, no, I don't want to inconvenience you like that, but— It's just that—okay, okay. I'm sorry. Of course, yes, of course.
>*He hangs up.*
He wants to meet us.

RONNIE
Whata you mean?

JOEY
He didn't want to talk on the phone. He didn't want to discuss our problem on the phone, because nothing is safe anymore.

RONNIE
So he wants to meet us? What about?

JOEY
There's a place he likes. He didn't name it, but I know it. It's on the corner.
>*Joey starts off down left, but Ronnie lags back.*

RONNIE
What corner?

JOEY
Don't worry what corner. It's not far. Just a few blocks from here.

RONNIE
Why do I have to go?
>*Retreating to the lamppost.*
I don't wanna go, Joey.

JOEY
You're comin', Ronnie. We discussed you would help me out for the money you owed me.

RONNIE
I did my part.

JOEY
I still need help.

RONNIE
I don't wanna do no more.

JOEY
Stalking Ronnie.
What am I gonna do, let you go warn your friend? Do I look like a jerkoff in your eyes here? Can you concentrate? Look at me! Huh? Tell me.

RONNIE
Warn him what?

JOEY
Ready to go.
Let's go.

RONNIE
I wouldn't warn him. I don't wanna warn him.

JOEY
Why not? He's your friend.

RONNIE
I wanna go home. I'm tired.

JOEY
So he's not your friend anymore. Is that the line of shit you're trying to entertain me with here? I mean you are strictly Cable Access, Ronnie.

RONNIE

That's what I'm saying.

JOEY

Because if he is not your friend, then I must be your friend. And even if I'm not—even if you're nobody's friend, who cares. You're coming with me because we have a deal and because I say so.

With that things are settled, and Joey turns to go.

RONNIE

I wanna ask you one thing, okay.

JOEY

You comin' or not?

RONNIE

Yes, yes, but—

JOEY

My uncle's gonna be waitin'. You don't wanna keep my uncle Malvolio waitin'.

RONNIE

I know that. But as a favor. Just one thing.

JOEY

What? Tell me the favor.

RONNIE

I just want to ask you that you don't tell your uncle I gloated.

JOEY

So you admit it.

RONNIE

No, no, that's—

JOEY

I just heard you, Ronnie.

RONNIE

I'm saying I did whatever I did which you mistook for gloating. I did that. And as a result you think I gloated. That's what I'm saying—you think I gloated, so you might say I did. That'd be only natural—you think it, so you say it, even though I didn't. I'm asking you not to.

JOEY

I can't promise that.

RONNIE

Why?

JOEY

Shoving Ronnie ahead of him.
You don't fucking give up, do you Ronnie?

RONNIE

I didn't gloat, Joey. You know I didn't.

> *Music as lights fade out on Joey and Ronnie walking off.*
> *TOMMY STONES, a large man in a black full-length*
> *leather jacket, enters carrying a park bench, which he sets*
> *down a little left of center. Then he moves off as the lights*
> *rise, bringing night, moonlight, a park as Tommy Stones re-*
> *turns pushing a wheelchair with UNCLE MALVOLIO*
> *seated in it. He wears pajamas and a sweater, and a blanket*
> *covers his lap. They settle stage right of the bench, and*
> *Tommy Stones looks around. He's on guard duty, while*
> *Uncle Malvolio looks up, more or less directly over his*
> *head, searching for something in the night sky. Tommy*
> *notes Uncle Malvolio's action and joins him, the two of*
> *them searching high in the night sky. Then, as the music*

*fades out, Joey and Ronnie enter, Ronnie coming in along
the wall, staying as close to it as he can, lagging back.*

JOEY

Hello, Uncle Mal.

UNCLE MALVOLIO

Hello, Joey. What the hell is going on here?
Looking up again.
Where's the moon? I come out, I like to see the moon. Where is it?

JOEY

The moon?

UNCLE MALVOLIO

Yeah.

JOEY
Searching the sky, too.
I don't know.

UNCLE MALVOLIO

Do you suppose it's hiding, or just trying to make things darker
than they need be?

JOEY

Well, it's cloudy.

UNCLE MALVOLIO
Glaring at Ronnie.
This guy is with you, Joey? Or is he just some bum lurking around
where he has no business?!

TOMMY STONES
Taking a step toward Ronnie.
You wanna move it, buddy.

RONNIE
I'm with him.
Inching toward Joey, but staying behind the park bench.

JOEY
Oh, hey! Ronnie's with me. Tell 'em you're with me, Ronnie.

RONNIE
I just did.

UNCLE MALVOLIO
What about you, Ronnie? You like the moon in or out?

RONNIE
Ahhhhh.
Looking up.

UNCLE MALVOLIO
These guys, Tommy, neither one of them ever thought about it.

TOMMY STONES
You should think about it.

RONNIE
Like he says, it's cloudy.

UNCLE MALVOLIO
Oh. You think that's what it is? It's cloudy.

JOEY
It could be something else, but we have no idea.

UNCLE MALVOLIO
You know what! The hell with it! Let's not indulge! Let's not wallow! I'm a hard guy, right, Tommy. I can do without.

TOMMY STONES
Of course.

UNCLE MALVOLIO
It won't be the first time.

JOEY
It's great to see you, Uncle Mal.

UNCLE MALVOLIO
What for? I look like a trash bag. This gettin' old ain't for sissies.
Somebody shoulda warned me.

JOEY
I heard you were having some health problems, Uncle Mal, and I
regret having to bother you, but—

UNCLE MALVOLIO
No, no, I'm talking about boredom for crissake. I'm talking about
I got less to do, and what I do have don't hold the same interest for
me it used to. So a call like the one you made is a bolt out of the
blue in as much as I have no fucking idea what might be the content of what you are calling me about. What the hell could Joey
have to tell me? That's what I'm sayin' to myself, you see, so there
is for a minute this actual kind of time period in which I don't
know—I am in doubt and—
> Suddenly to Ronnie, who is clutching the back of park
> bench.
Hey, Ronnie, could you relax! Take a breath!
> To Joey.
Joey, he's a nervous wreck, this Ronnie you brought me here. Is he
on your side of this mess you're in or not?

JOEY
Ohh, definitely, yeah.

UNCLE MALVOLIO
So why does he look like he done something he wishes he hadn't and his balls are shriveling up because he knows I'm gonna catch him? What's your last name?

RONNIE
My name? Why?

UNCLE MALVOLIO
Who the hell is this asshole, Joey, he gives me back talk?!!

TOMMY STONES
Why is because he asked you!

JOEY
Tell him your goddamn last name, Ronnie!

RONNIE
Ronnie Birnbaum.

UNCLE MALVOLIO
That's not your last name.

RONNIE
Yeah, sure it is. That's it. Ronnie Birnbaum.

UNCLE MALVOLIO
Ronnie's your first name. I asked for your last name.

TOMMY STONES
Be specific, asshole.

RONNIE
Birnbaum.

UNCLE MALVOLIO
So you're Ronnie Birnbaum.

To Tommy Stones.
Tommy, this is Ronnie Birnbaum.

TOMMY STONES
Is that right?

JOEY
You heard of him, Uncle Mal?

UNCLE MALVOLIO
I have now. Oh, the hell with it. You know, guess what? If we don't
get this thing in gear, I'm gonna have to take a piss before we even
get our money on the table—let's at least get started—I got this
prostate bullshit going on—it's a disgrace—

JOEY
I heard. I was sorry to hear. You're okay, though.

UNCLE MALVOLIO
I'm fine except I gotta piss more than a pregnant woman and I got
this radioactive implant up my ass. Other than that, I'm fine. So
what I wanna know is enough with the niceties, let's drop the fucking hammer. Why are we here talking?

JOEY
You mean, about why I called? This is about Teresa.

UNCLE MALVOLIO
How's she doin'?

JOEY
Well, some guy—this guy—

UNCLE MALVOLIO
Not Birnbaum here!

RONNIE

No, no.

JOEY

A friend of his.

RONNIE

Let me just—could I say something here about this guy we're talking about, and that he is no longer anyone I would call a friend after what he done, which has more or less changed my mind about him to the degree that we are finished.

UNCLE MALVOLIO

So what did this guy do? It must be horrendous—you're willing to bother me—poor Birnbaum here is done with the guy. I can't wait to find out what the hell atrocity did he commit.

JOEY

That's what I'm coming to, Uncle Mal, because it's not an easy thing to explain, but this guy— Ray is his name, and somehow he got ahold of Teresa and he ran this scam on her, so she, you know—

UNCLE MALVOLIO

What's his last name?

JOEY

I don't know his last name.
To Ronnie.
Did you tell me his last name?

RONNIE

It's Matz.

UNCLE MALVOLIO

Matz. What kinda name is that?

TOMMY STONES
It could be shortened from something.

UNCLE MALVOLIO
Like what?

TOMMY STONES
Something longer. Like from maybe one of the former Soviet sat-
ellites, or the Balkans, maybe.

UNCLE MALVOLIO
You mean like Matz-inski or Matz-usiwick, or something like that,
so he's Polish or Czech or Russian.

TOMMY STONES
Yeah. Rumanian.

UNCLE MALVOLIO
Is that the case here, Birnbaum?

JOEY
You know, Uncle Mal, if you gimme the floor for just a second, I
can lay things out so the obvious point is his background is irrele-
vant, if you wanna know what I think, because what he done to
Teresa is not something to be mitigated no matter what kind of
backward origins he might have.
Sitting down on the bench, he faces Uncle Malvolio.
They don't matter. She makes a mistake, you know, she ends up in
bed with this jerkoff. You know, she ain't little Teresa anymore, I
gotta say it, facts are facts, she's a grown woman. And it don't
matter she's immature or not, and pigheaded, she don't give me
ten cents for anything I say to her—I try to advise her, but she
don't listen—so she goes home with this guy. Not that I know him,
and could have advised against it, and not that she would have listened anyway—so they are in the sack, doin' whatever—we all
know how that goes—no need to dwell on it, I don't even want to
think about it, except I have to, because this guy has a dog, and

you know— So what! Right?! Everybody knows somebody, they have a dog! But the next thing I know is Teresa comes to me, and she's sobbing, she's hysterical, because evidently the dog is in the bed—the bed while they're slammin' away—the guy and the dog too, that's what she tells me.

Getting up, ready to show what happened.

So I look him up—after she tells me—this Ray, I look him up, and this is where Ronnie comes in, Ronnie knows the guy, Ronnie owes me some money, so I tell Ronnie I gotta talk to the guy—so Ronnie—

UNCLE MALVOLIO

Wait a minute, wait a minute! Go back! What about in the bed? The dog in the bed. This is what you're saying? The dog is involved!

Looking up to Tommy Stones.

This is interesting. Ray Matz from wherever is workin' Teresa over with his pile driver, the next thing she knows, there's this furry creature gettin' in on the action.

JOEY

That's what she says.

UNCLE MALVOLIO

Doin' what?

JOEY

Who?

UNCLE MALVOLIO

The dog. What's he doin'?

JOEY

What's the dog doin'? You wanna know what's the dog doin'?

UNCLE MALVOLIO

Yeah.

JOEY

I don't know. I mean exactly.

UNCLE MALVOLIO

What'd she say?

JOEY

That she wanted something done to the guy. I hadda do something! So I got ahold of Ronnie, because—

UNCLE MALVOLIO

What kinda dog?

JOEY

What?

UNCLE MALVOLIO

You never met this dog?

JOEY

Ronnie, what kinda dog is it?

RONNIE

I don't know. I think he's— Well mainly, he's a mutt.

UNCLE MALVOLIO

What's his name?

JOEY

What's the dog's name? Ronnie, what's the dog's name?

UNCLE MALVOLIO

Does he have a name? He gotta have a name.

RONNIE

Well, sure. I guess. He must. I'm sure he does, but I don't know what it is.

UNCLE MALVOLIO
So what is it?

RONNIE
I don't know. That's what I'm sayin'. I don't know his name.

UNCLE MALVOLIO
You met the dog, though. You seen him.

RONNIE
Yeah, sure.

JOEY
So you probably heard his name.

UNCLE MALVOLIO
But you can't think of it.

TOMMY STONES
Maybe it'll come to you.

UNCLE MALVOLIO
What's he look like? Is he a big dog?

RONNIE
Pretty big.

UNCLE MALVOLIO
So what does he do?

RONNIE
Do? What does the dog do? Well, he hangs out, you know, with Ray. He's Ray's dog, you know, so he—

UNCLE MALVOLIO
No, no! I mean when he's in bed with Teresa. That's what I'm tryin' to get at here, Joey, what does he do then?

JOEY

I didn't ask her, you know exactly. I didn't wanna pry.

UNCLE MALVOLIO

Weren't you curious?

JOEY

I didn't want to pry, you know. Maybe I should have asked.

UNCLE MALVOLIO

I think you should have. Because what we got here, is a ménage à trois, right, except the third party ain't a human being. You ever done that? I gotta tell you, it's a goddamn roller-coaster ride—it's a regular fun house! It was all three humans in my case and I was young, I was very young, you gotta be young. There's a certain amount of awkwardness, some kind of preliminary bullshit where everybody's gotta figure out who does what when, maybe some-body's shy, you give 'em a little time, but once everybody manages to put their difficulties behind them, the whole thing can be a load of fun. You gotta be young though. And you can't have any radio-active implants embedded up your ass.

JOEY

I mean, Uncle Mal, you're right, I shoulda asked for more details, and I will, but the real trouble with this guy ain't what he done to her, anyway, but what he did to me.

UNCLE MALVOLIO

He done something to you, too?

JOEY

That's what I'm getting at— I confront the guy, right, I got a gun on him—
Pacing, acting it out behind the bench.
I want him to think I will take him out maybe on the basis of nothin' more substantial than a fucking mood shift, you know! That's what I want him to think, but—

UNCLE MALVOLIO
But you don't do it. You don't take him out.

JOEY
No. Never without permission.

UNCLE MALVOLIO
Even with permission, you wouldn't have the concrete balls to do that. Would you? Hey, don't even think about it. Don't even try and answer. Don't bother yourself. Let's be honest. All right?

JOEY
All right.

UNCLE MALVOLIO
You got nothin' to prove in this area. Anyway, you're tryin' to prove something, you prove nothing. The point for you is you're just trying to impress this asshole that he's in danger. So that he looks at what he done in a serious light. Am I right? That's what you want.

JOEY
Exactly, Uncle Mal. But the problem is, I ain't sure he takes the whole thing seriously—that he sees in any way the seriousness of what he done. I mean, Ronnie's there, he's my witness to what the guy does, and— Tell him, Ronnie. Tell him what he does.

RONNIE
What?
Looking to Joey, seeking instruction.

TOMMY STONES
Tell us what this guy does.
His back to Uncle Malvolio, Joey mouths the words "He gloats."

RONNIE
He gloats. The guy gloats.

UNCLE MALVOLIO
Wait a minute! You got your piece in this guy's face, Joey, and he gloats?
Enraged.
This is what he thinks of you?! This is what you let him get away with? You shoulda shot him!

JOEY
No, no, he don't gloat.

TOMMY STONES
So Birnbaum is lying here?

RONNIE
Sure, Joey. Remember you says—

JOEY
He don't gloat. You're the one.
Grabbing Ronnie.
He gloated.

UNCLE MALVOLIO
Birnbaum gloated?! He's the one!

RONNIE
No, no.

JOEY
The fuck you didn't. Admit it.

RONNIE
Still in the headlock.
I'm with Joey, right. He's got a gun. If I'm gloating, which I don't even know about, it's because I'm on Joey's side. We got the gun.

UNCLE MALVOLIO
This is why I put you to work in the fucking fish store!
Raging at Joey, charging at him in the wheelchair.
Everything you touch turns into The Three fucking Stooges. How could you let this happen?

JOEY
Releasing Ronnie.
That's why I come to you—I couldn't let it go.
Dropping to his knees before Uncle Malvolio.
I couldn't let it go. Ask Ronnie if I could let it go. I couldn't, could I, Ronnie?

RONNIE
Backed up against the Dumpster.
No, no, he couldn't let it go.

JOEY
I come to you. I hadda. Look at me, I'm all twisted up in knots.

UNCLE MALVOLIO
Wheeling away.
You want me to shoot him? Is that what you want?

JOEY
No, no, I'm not telling you what to do.

UNCLE MALVOLIO
I think that's what you want. Maybe I will, maybe I won't.

JOEY
I'm telling you what happened is all.

UNCLE MALVOLIO
In order that I do what?

JOEY

Whatever you want.

UNCLE MALVOLIO

So as far as your expectations, what are they?

JOEY

I just want to supply you with the facts and then I'm totally comfortable with you do whatever you think is right.

UNCLE MALVOLIO

Wheeling on, thinking, he ends up back near the bench.

Which I have no idea what that is. What I think is right could turn out to be any number of things. You got this goddamn dog problem, now you bring it to me. Teresa is what? A lota flashbacks, she's post-traumatic?

JOEY

I don't know. I don't think so.

UNCLE MALVOLIO

How's her memory? Is it repressed, or she knows what happened, she knows what she tol' you?

JOEY

I would say so.

UNCLE MALVOLIO

She should watch some of those daytime talk shows—there's people on every one of them getting catharsis and some other kind of uplifting crap. Maybe that's what she needs. Tell her I said so. How did you last leave her? You know what I thought when I saw her two, three months ago? She's going to be *Penthouse*—this little toaster oven is *Playboy*—if she gets half a break. Where was it I saw her, Tommy?

TOMMY STONES
This was at Bernardo's in the afternoon, she was having lunch with some blonde.

UNCLE MALVOLIO
Right, that's right. The atmosphere was steamy—the room, I mean, the actual air was hot just from her sittin' there oblivious, yappin' away about God knows what, her shoes, her panties, her nail polish, who knows what, but there's this halo around her. It's oozing, you know.

TOMMY STONES
Her aura.

UNCLE MALVOLIO
That's right. Her aura. Sexy.

TOMMY STONES
Very sexy.

UNCLE MALVOLIO
We both felt it.

TOMMY STONES
Very sexy.

UNCLE MALVOLIO
So, Birnbaum!
    At the sound of his name, Ronnie startles, looks to see what he should do, then Tommy snaps his fingers at Ronnie.

TOMMY STONES
He wants you.
    Ronnie hurries over to Uncle Malvolio.

UNCLE MALVOLIO

We got our dog problem—we gotta do something, right? We got this dog, he's a problem. Here's what we'll do— You go down to the corner there and use the pay phone. You get Ray Matz on the pay phone, and tell him to meet you on the corner. Some other corner, but not too far. What in fact will happen is Tommy will be hangin' around and he will ambush this fuckhead when he shows up—he can kick him around, give him a smack in the mouth, maybe break a finger or two, crack a rib and then when he's done pukin', Tommy can present him with his situation as we see it: he should not have gloated. But since he did these are his options. Number one— somebody's gotta die—it could be him, or it could be—

He gestures for everyone to come near. They all lean in attentively.

Now listen closely. I'm thinking it could be the dog. Since he's the problem, why not? But we don't care. It's Ray Matz's choice. But either he eats a bullet, or the dog takes the fall into Hell in his place. You got that? It's up to him.

JOEY

I got a cell phone he could use right here, Uncle Mal.

UNCLE MALVOLIO

No, no.

JOEY

He's got one. He's got his own, if—

Joey and Ronnie both pull out their cell phones.

UNCLE MALVOLIO

Do you fucking morons pay no attention to the kind of world we are living in?! You don't do nothing on those things! The whole world can listen in, you might as well walk up and down the street shouting your secrets—they suck them right out of the air—they don't even need a bug. When I say, "PAY PHONE!" I MEAN, "PAY PHONE!!"

Raging, he slams his fists on the arms of his wheelchair.

RONNIE
You're right, you're right about pay phones. But what do I say to him? He's not gonna come out on my say-so after what happened!

UNCLE MALVOLIO
Tommy, help him out!
    Tommy Stones moves to Ronnie.

TOMMY STONES
Yeah, sure. Ronnie, Ronnie, together we can do this thing. This is something I know about. Don't waste another second worrying about this thing.
    With his arm around Ronnie, he ushers him away.
Listen to me, count on me. I do this all the time.

RONNIE
You do what?

TOMMY STONES
I get people to go places they shouldn't. Like right now it could be that you are on your way someplace you should never go.
    They walk from the park, and then Uncle Malvolio turns to Joey.

UNCLE MALVOLIO
Everything okay with you now, Joey?

JOEY
Yeah, yeah.

UNCLE MALVOLIO
You mind I take a piss?

JOEY
No, no. Whatever you say, Uncle Mal.
    Uncle Mal gets to his feet with Joey's assistance.

It's very generous of you, everything you're doing. It's more than I could've asked for is what I think, Uncle Mal.

> *As Joey helps him, Uncle Mal makes his way up toward the dumpster.*

UNCLE MALVOLIO

That's what you think. But do you know what? I don't know what I think about this whole thing here. I ain't come to any firm conclusions yet.

> *At the dumpster, Joey lifts the lid of one of the trash cans and looks away, as Uncle Malvolio starts to piss.*

Other than you should understand it's not a possibility that I am going to in reality authorize this guy gets whacked over what you brought us here.

> *As the piss rattles into the trash can.*

Maybe he gloats, maybe he doesn't. It could happen. Maybe he insults you, I don't know. I wasn't there.

> *Finished now, fixing his pajama bottoms, wiping his fingers.*

Without a doubt, Tommy will slam this smart mouth around a little, but nobody's gonna get popped over such a thing. It would be ridiculous.

> *On his way back to the wheelchair, he stops.*

What we gotta do is make him give up the dog. That's what we can pin our hopes on. If we can make him betray the dog, as long as he lives, it's gonna bother him. If you're gonna try and do harm to people, Joey, you might as well get them deep, you know, twist their fucking souls if you can! And that's what this could be if we were fortunate enough to pull it off. Because we would know but he wouldn't that he wasn't really gonna die—and that's where the real fun will be ours, because we'll know—and one day we can tell him—that he betrayed the dog for nothing but a dream—this fucking fairy tale of bullshit fear we have inflicted on him. So he betrays his friend without a reason except he's afraid to die.

> *Settling back in the chair.*

Does that sound like what you were looking for?

JOEY
Whatever you think.

UNCLE MALVOLIO
I guess that's what I think. Listen, could you do me a favor?

JOEY
What? Of course.

UNCLE MALVOLIO
Tommy's gonna be busy with Birnbaum, etcetera. Could you
wheel me home? I wanna go home. I need a push.

JOEY
I'd be happy to, Uncle Mal. I'd be honored.

UNCLE MALVOLIO
You can probably, if you hurry, get back in time to get a couple
smacks in on this Ray, if that interests you.

JOEY
*Pulling the wheelchair back, in order to start off with
Uncle Malvolio.*
Yeah, yeah, that's what I'll do.

UNCLE MALVOLIO
Suddenly pointing up.
See the moon?! Now it comes out! Sure. Look at it, peeking out—
sticking its sissy nose out from behind the clouds!
Yelling up.
Go back where you came from! Go on! GET OUTA HERE!
He looks to Joey.
No, no, I like the moon.
*He smiles up to the moon and gestures as if the moon is
cowering above him.*
It's okay. I was just kidding. You can stay.
Music as they wheel off upstage. The lights cross fade and

Ronnie appears, moving near the lamppost where he paces a beat before Ray enters, walking toward him.

RAY
Hey, Ronnie.

RONNIE
Where's the dog? I tol' you to bring the dog.

RAY
I know what you told me.

RONNIE
Where is he?

RAY
He was sleepin'. He ain't comin'.

RONNIE
I tol' you to bring him. You said you would.

RAY
Don't you wanna know why I come? Aren't you wondering?

RONNIE
Is he back at your place?

RAY
Whata you care?

RONNIE
I wanna know.

RAY
I mean, I don't have to do everything you tell me, you know, Ronnie. Not everything. In fact, if the truth be told, the only

reason I showed myself at this moment is because it was eatin' at me—

Grabbing Ronnie by the shirtfront and backing him
downstage left, his fist raised in a threat.

I oughta break your nose for what you done to me. I oughta separate you from some of your teeth, because as things stand, you are unscathed, you are—

Tommy Stones enters behind Ray.

TOMMY STONES
Hello, Ray.

RAY
Yeah.
Looking at Tommy Stones.
Do I know you?
To Ronnie.
Who's this?

RONNIE
He's talkin' to you. Not me. He ain't talkin' to me.

RAY
Oh, no. Not again. You didn't do it to me again! Did you do it again, Ronnie, you asshole?

TOMMY STONES
Whata you say, Ray?
As Ray takes a step back, Joey hurries in behind him,
shoving him.

JOEY
What's the good word, smart mouth?!!

RAY
When am I gonna learn?

Ray feints running one way and tries to escape another, but Tommy Stones cuts him off. Ray backs up into Joey, who shoves him, and Tommy slams Ray in the mouth. Ray yelps, holding his nose, as Tommy grabs him by the hand, lays his hand on the top of the dumpster, and slashes the lid of a garbage can down on his fingers. Ray screams, recoils, dropping to his knees as Tommy Stones taunts him.

TOMMY STONES

Does it hurt, Ray?
Dogs are barking, a subway roars past nearby.
Give him a kick, Joey!
As Ray rolls on the ground, Joey lunges and kicks him in the stomach. Tommy grabs Ray by his injured hand and lifts him, shoving and following him off. Ronnie has retreated to the lamppost as Joey looks off after Ray and Tommy Stones. Joey bounces with the energy of the beating and pulls cigars from his pocket. He turns to Ronnie.

JOEY

You want a smoke? I got these excellent, extremely exclusive cigars—they are Habana Davidoff Number Ones. Fifty years in the making, all these cared-for and cultivated leaves mixed with the aroma of Commie-worker sweat.
Offering one to Ronnie.
This one's for you.

RONNIE

Yeah, I guess. Why not?
Taking the cigar.

JOEY

The only thing I got to ask you is, after you smoke it, you gotta vow to gimme the ring back. I want to save them all. Will you gimme your word on that?

RONNIE
Joey, listen, there's something I got to tell you.

JOEY
Yeah? What's that?

RONNIE
I probably should have done it before, but somehow it never seemed like the right moment.

JOEY
But now it does.

RONNIE
Anyway, what the fuck—you should know that I have psychic powers.

JOEY
Who? You?

RONNIE
Yeah.

JOEY
But you're a joke.

RONNIE
Well, maybe. It's not something I can count on, or you know, just summon up on demand.
Joey, amused and dismissive, shakes his head and starts away.
Because they just come over me, these psychic powers, like a wave, all these thoughts about people and what they done. Like you—
This stops Joey.
—you were married long ago, weren't you?

JOEY

No.

RONNIE

How many times you been married?

JOEY

Returning, annoyed.

I never been married.

RONNIE

You never been married?

JOEY

No.

RONNIE

Never?

JOEY

I had some girlfriends.

RONNIE

No, no it's more than girlfriends. What am I doin' here? I'm messin' it up. Maybe I'm thinking too much, maybe I'm showing off. Because what I'm getting off you is about this woman, and she's in love with you!

JOEY

What woman?

RONNIE

And I'm getting this old apartment building on the corner and you are a kid on the fire escape—you're climbing up and you're going one two three four five six—

Stopping, realizing.

You're a kid! A kid! So of course you couldn't be married. But it's that kind of love—that's what mixed me up, because if you coulda married this woman, you woulda. But you're a kid, see, and it's six—no, five stories to this window with white curtains on it, white curtains with apples pictured on faded cloth, faded apples, faded curtains and leaves— It's all fucking faded.

Facing Joey.

Where is this? What am I seeing?

JOEY

Keep going!

RONNIE

There's a woman inside and you want to go see her, you want to visit her, but you're afraid. I don't know why you're afraid. It's because of something—I mean somebody else, not her, but her husband. Except he isn't really her husband. I mean, you didn't know that then, but you do now—he was just this man, who was in her house all the time and he hated you, but he isn't home. You could have come up the front way and knocked, but you're trying to see in to find out if he's there, and you make a noise and you hide. You're ashamed of sneaking and afraid of the man and you don't want anybody to see you, so you back up into the shadows. And she sticks her head out, but she doesn't see you. Her hair is red, it's tangled, all tangled. Long. Falling down around her shoulders. She's got something in her hand, it's a—rosary—white with big beads, and she drops it as she looks out, and she reaches, and loses her balance, reaching for the rosary, spinning through the air, and she follows it. She grabs at the air and turns in the air, and she sees you. She sees you and your eyes meet and she says your name, she says, "Joey," and she sees you standing there watching—

His fingers fall from the lamppost like a tiny figure falling.

As she drops down into the dark of the alley below. Who was that, Joey?

Joey turns, moves toward the dumpster.

Do you know who that was?

JOEY
Leaning on the dumpster.
Yeah. I know.

RONNIE
Who?

JOEY
My aunt Irene.

RONNIE
See. See what I mean?

JOEY
Yeah. How did you do that?

RONNIE
I didn't do it. The spooks did it? They got stuff they want said, so they come after me. So they're tellin' me stuff I don't know anything about, and then I'm tellin' it to you, and it's stuff you already know.
He starts to go.
That's what I can't figure out. That's my question.
Looking skyward, and walking away.
Excuse me, but fuck me. What good does that do anybody?

JOEY
Who you talking to? Ronnie, who the fuck you talking to?
Joey looks after Ronnie, then turns his eyes upward.
Music and lights going to black, as Joey drifts offstage,
and Tommy Stones brings out a bench and sets it down-
stage. The lights rise on Ray entering with the DOG on
a leash. His face is bruised; he limps a little. He carries a
bottle of whiskey in one hand, a large paper bag in the
other. Inside the bag is a dog bowl, a box of dog cookies.
He walks up to the park bench, and the dog climbs onto

*the bench. Ray sits down beside him. Music out, lights
brighten on the whole park.*

RAY

This is one hell of a thing we got ourselves into. I never saw it
coming, you know. I don't even know what happened there with
Teresa that night. You were there, I was there. Everybody's rollin'
around on the bed. Now this. You want a drink? I'm gonna have
one.
He takes a drink.
One, hell, I think it's gonna be more than one. Because it's you or
me, they say. You wanna biscuit?
*He takes out a red bowl, drops it to the floor, then pulls out
a box of dog cookies.*
I gotta handle this thing. I wanna handle it, but I don't know
how.
Giving the dog a cookie.
These guys mean business, you know. That's the problem. There's
no explainin' anything to them. What was it, huh? All the hullaba-
loo of what me and her were up to? All the yellin' and carryin' on,
and the smells and everything—you couldn't resist.
He gives the dog another cookie.
You're big on smells, right? It looks like wrestlin', looks like a dog
pile, you hadda join in. Is that what it was, you crazy fuck? It looks
like fun. You always been crazy, you know.
He grabs the dog by the neck, rubbing, squeezing, loving.
Like that time you ate all the Brillo Pads. Or the way you want to
drink my piss right out of the air on its way from my dick to the
toilet. I mean, what's that all about, huh? Maybe you could ex-
plain that one to me.
He drinks.
Or that time you stole the lamb chop right off the kitchen counter!
I turn my back for one second, next thing I know, where's the lamb
chop? And you mighta got away with it except, no, you gotta act
guilty—you give yourself away the minute I look at you.
He drinks.

Or like when I learned how to train you to do "off" from that trainer, and you would sniff the piece of hot dog in my fist—

Teasing the dog with a dog treat in his fist.

—and then when you backed off because you couldn't get it, I would say the word "off" and give you the hot dog! And you bought the whole scam. All for a hot dog. You clown. You fucking dumbo. Like when I was trimmin' your toenails and I cut the one too short and it bled and you squealed and yelled at me, but you bore me no grudge.

Takes a drink.

I mean, maybe they wouldn't really shoot me. But how do I find out, because they do kill people! So I say, okay kill me but don't hurt the dog, and they do it, then what? I'm dead and stuck in some fucking landfill. You see my problem? It's maybe what you would do. But you don't look down on me. You don't have an attitude toward me that he's a human being so I am superior, I am going to look down on him. The way people do, I mean, looking down on you because you are a dog. He's a fucking animal.

He takes a drink.

Remember the time you ate my checkbook? I mean, why? You had chew toys all over the fucking place. You don't have a clue what I'm talking about, do you? You're just listenin' to my stupid voice and hopin' for another cookie. Who knows what you would do if it were your choice? But it ain't. You don't have the choice. I do. I mean, you just love me and that's it for you. But people ain't like that. I mean, people are different. I mean, people suck. They suck.

Tommy Stones has entered from up right, and Ray sees him moving closer.

They just suck. They suck, you know. People suck.

TOMMY STONES
Standing, looking down at Ray and the Dog.
Who's it gonna be? I mean, who we kiddin' here, huh? But you gotta say it. You gotta say it's one or the other. "It's me." Or, "The dog dies."

Ray extends his arm with the leash for Tommy to take.
Say it! Who dies?

RAY
The dog dies.
    Tommy Stones takes the leash and walks the dog off up-stage right, leaving Ray sitting, watching. From another angle, up left and behind Ray, TERESA enters. She's in her early twenties. Very sexy in a tight skirt, colorful blouse. She walks up behind Ray.

TERESA
How are you, Ray?

RAY
    Startled, he looks and sees her.
Hello, Teresa.

TERESA
Hello, Ray.
    Studying him.
How's everything?

RAY
Oh, you know. Not so bad.

TERESA
You don't look so good. Somethin' happen?

RAY
Something's always happening, Teresa. You know that.

TERESA
Well, sure.

RAY
Sometimes we know about it, sometimes we don't.

TERESA
Easing up behind him, she touches his hair.
Did you fall down the stairs, or something?

RAY
Actually, I got the shit beat out of me.

TERESA
Yeah? Did you make somebody mad?

RAY
I guess I did, Teresa.

TERESA
Do you need some cheering up?
She hangs her purse on the end of the bench.
Maybe I could cheer you up.

RAY
I don't think so.

TERESA
I bet I could.
Joining him on the bench.

RAY
How would you do that?

TERESA
Sliding closer, touching his chest.
Well, how do you think?

RAY
I don't know.

TERESA
Her fingers slip inside his shirt.
I was thinking, you know, we could screw. I could go down on you
or something. Would you like that?

RAY
They're going to shoot my dog.

TERESA
I heard that. That's why I was thinking you could maybe use some
fun. Whata you think?
She strokes his thigh.
I could do something right here, maybe. If you wanted.

RAY
You mean, we could screw right here, right now?

TERESA
Sure. You know, so you could forget about everything.
Her hand slides along his thigh.
So you could feel good.
Kissing his ear, his cheek.
Wouldn't you like to forget about everything?

RAY
Turning to her.
Yeah. I would.

TERESA
So lemme help you.
*They kiss, then part quickly. He looks at her and they kiss
again, as he touches her blouse.*

RAY
It wouldn't bring my dog back to life, though, would it?

TERESA
No, he'd still get killed.

RAY
He wouldn't come back to life.

TERESA
No. He would stay dead.
As Ray moves his hand to her breast.
But you would feel good. Don't you feel kind of good already?

RAY
Yeah. Well, I feel something.

TERESA
Sure. Me, too.

RAY
He kisses her.
I don't know if it's good, though.

TERESA
I think it is.

RAY
I don't know why you did this, Teresa. You instigated this whole thing. Didn't you?

TERESA
Whata you mean, what whole thing?

RAY
My dog is getting whacked because of you. That's what I mean.

TERESA
I don't wanna talk about the dog.

Unzipping his fly, she eases down.

RAY
But why would you do such a thing?

TERESA
C'mon, Ray.

RAY
Why would you want him to die like this?

TERESA
You wanna shut up about the dog!
She stands up.
We can go over to my house. Or your house, I don't care.
Moving toward her purse.

RAY
You can stop it. You can tell 'em to stop it.
He grabs her arm, stopping her before she gets the purse.

TERESA
They ain't gonna listen to me.
Pulling free.

RAY
Rising, going to her.
He's just a poor fucking dog. I saw him in the window of the pet store, you know. He was looking out at me. He was looking right at me through the glass. I went in and I got him. That was six years ago. I had him six years. Six years, Teresa.

TERESA
How big a jerk are you, Ray? Can you answer me that?

RAY

I just don't know why you gotta have him assassinated. What'd he do?

TERESA

The hell with you.
Charging away.
That's all you ever care about is your stupid dog?
Kicking the dog bowl.

RAY

What are you doin'? What the hell are you doin'?

TERESA

She drops onto the bench.
You think you can treat people any which way, don't you? Well, you can't!

RAY

What way?

TERESA

People! Some girl comes over to your house—she gives you everything she's got, she gives you the ride of your life, you're thinking about the dog. You're not even thinking about her. You're with her, you're in bed with her, but you're thinking about the dog.

RAY

What are you talking about?
Warily he sits beside her.
I don't know what you're talking about!

TERESA

Anybody can see it. It's in your eyes.
He's trying to touch her, but she keeps pushing his hands away.

The way you look at that dog. The look you give him.
    Realizing.
You love that dog. You're humping the girl, but you don't love her,
you love the dog.

RAY

I never met you before that night. We barely knew each other,
Teresa. We just met.

TERESA

You think that matters!

RAY

I picked you up in a bar.

TERESA

Don't you insult me now.

RAY

It's not an insult. It's a fact.

TERESA

It's a fact and an insult. People have their limits.
    On her feet, ready to leave, this time she gets her purse.
They can only take so much. Maybe the next time you'll remember
this and think about what I'm telling you.

RAY

But what are you telling me? I don't know what you're telling me!

TERESA

People have feelings, and you better remember it.

RAY

Dogs have feelings, too. So do dogs.

TERESA
Bullshit!

RAY
They do. They have feelings and things they want and things they think about and things they like and don't like.

TERESA
No. I don't care. You have got to learn your lesson.

RAY
What lesson? I don't know what this lesson is.

TERESA
I think you do.

RAY
No. I have no fucking idea.
From offstage, a gunshot. Ray freezes, looks off.

TERESA
Have some consideration. You should have some fucking consideration.
She walks off up left. Ray stares in the direction of the shot. He moves and looks out around the corner of the wall, and then he hurries back to the bench, as Tommy Stones strides in lugging a garbage bag. He walks in front of the bench, facing Ray. He lowers the garbage bag to the ground.

TOMMY STONES
You want him? I got a dog of my own.
Tommy is cold and fatalistic.
This was a nice dog. I could see that. You probably loved him, even though things worked out the way they did.
He walks to Ray, almost confrontational.
You can bury him if you want. You got a yard, or you know some-

body with a yard, you could bury him in their yard. Or you could go to the veterinarian over on Thompson, it's just above Canal, a few doors up from the corner. East side of the street. They will cremate the dog for you. You can have his ashes. I think that's what I'll do with my dog. You could do that.

> *Ray is unresponsive, and Tommy, looking around, comes up with another alternative.*

Or I could just toss him in the dumpster over there.

> *He bends as if to pick the bag up.*

RAY
No, no, I'll do it.

TOMMY STONES
Yeh? It's your call.

RAY
> *Reaching, he grabs on to the bag.*

I'll do it.

TOMMY STONES
Whatever you say.

> *As Ray sits on the bench, holding on to the bag.*

I was careful with him. It was quick. He didn't see it coming. You can tell yourself he didn't feel a thing.

RAY
Yeh. I'll do that.

TOMMY STONES
Sure, why not? I'll see you around.

> *Tommy heads off and Ray sits alone, then opens the top of the bag and peers in. From down right, Ronnie enters.*

RONNIE
Hey, Ray.

> ### RAY
> *He shuts the bag, a little embarrassed, then makes a joke mocking Tommy.*

The guy says I can tell myself he didn't feel a thing. I can also tell myself that I am a very high-ranking corporate executive. I can tell myself a lota crap.

> ### RONNIE

Don't torture yourself, Ray.

> ### RAY

I'm not torturing myself.
> *He takes a drink of whiskey.*

I'm just sayin' he felt it. Let's at least stick with the facts. This goddamn bullet smashing into his brain. He hadda feel something.

> ### RONNIE

The guy was just trying to be helpful, Ray.

> ### RAY

Yeh, I know. But let's be honest. We don't stick with the facts, where are we?

> ### RONNIE
> *Joining Ray on the bench.*

No, no, I wanna stick with the facts.

> ### RAY

It may not last very long, but it's gotta feel bad, that's all I'm saying.

> ### RONNIE

The guy was just trying to be helpful, that's all.

> ### RAY

I know. I know. I caught a break is the goddamn truth here. That's the truth.
> *Staring at the bag.*

Because the fact of the matter is that could be me in that goddamn bag.

RONNIE

That's what you gotta keep in the forefront of your thoughts here, Ray.

RAY

That's where it is. In the forefront!

RONNIE

That's the single most important fact here.
Nodding at the bag.
That could be you.

RAY

He was a nice dog, though.

RONNIE

Sure. Sure. Nobody's saying anything else. He was as good as they get.

RAY

But still just a dog.

RONNIE

That was the problem. For him, I mean. He was the dog.

RAY

Right. Right. I saved my fucking life.
He stands.
I used my head and saved my life.
He grabs the bag.
Good for me.
Ray lugs the bag to the dumpster. Ronnie watches Ray lift the bag onto the dumpster, open the lid, and shove the bag

*into the dumpster. He lowers the lid, leans against the
dumpster.*
You know what I'm gonna do, Ronnie?

      RONNIE
What?

      RAY
I'm gonna go look up Teresa.

      RONNIE
Yeh? What for, Ray?

      RAY
She owes me, that's what I think.

      RONNIE
Yeh?

      RAY
She owes me. Somebody owes me.

      RONNIE
Maybe.

      RAY
After goin' through all this—it's one hell of a thing to go through.
      Heading off.
I oughta at least get laid.
      *Music as Ronnie watches Ray go off up left. Then Ronnie
      turns out and sits there.*

      BLACKOUT

ACT TWO

*The larger aspects of the set remain: the concrete walls
and superstructure, the bricked-up painted loading dock
windows and grid. A wire street trash can sits in the corner
of the space previously dominated by the dumpster. The
area of the lamppost has been taken over by a kitchen unit:
a block of wallpapered wall with a lamp attached, shelves
full of tins, a wall phone. A kitchen table with two chairs
sits in front of the wall unit. The downstage right door has
had the sign removed from it so it now appears to be the
door to the apartment.*

*Music. Lights start up: in partial illumination, Teresa is
found with her arm ready to throw something, which she
throws; a glass rattles across the floor. The lights come up
full. She stands in front of the wall, and behind the table.
She wears a bathrobe, and having thrown the glass, she
looks off up left behind the wall, then grabs a tin canister,
which she slams on the tabletop. She opens it, roots in it,
slams it again. She grabs another tin canister, slams it on
the table, looks off again, and slams another canister. Ray
staggers in from the direction she has been looking; he
wears boxer shorts and a T-shirt.*

RAY
Whata you doin'?

TERESA
Whata you care?
She slams the canister back onto the shelf.

RAY
You're makin' a lot of noise.

TERESA
Go back to bed.
She grabs another canister, slams it, looks inside.

RAY

Are you lookin' for something? Can I help you?

TERESA

Opening a drawer, looking in.

No. I ain't lookin' for anything.

RAY

That's what it looks like you're doing, Teresa. It looks like you're looking for something.

TERESA

You wanna stop harassing me? Could you do that?

RAY

You woke me up.

TERESA

I would like a little privacy.

RAY

I mean, you do know that it's three o'clock in the morning? You do know that.

TERESA

Go back to bed, Ray.

She starts putting the canisters away, slamming them into place.

RAY

I'm awake now. I can't go back to sleep once I'm awake.

TERESA

I'm sorry, Ray. Go back to bed.

RAY

Just tell me what you're doing.

TERESA

Why?

Slamming a canister for punctuation.

RAY

Whata you mean "why?" You're my wife, you know— You're out here—

TERESA

So what?

Facing him.

RAY

So you're restless, you're worried and nasty! Because I'm risking life and limb, if I dare ask you a question, you sink your fucking teeth into me.

TERESA

So leave. I don't care.

RAY

Whata you mean, "leave"? Who said anything about leaving?

TERESA

I did.

RAY

Are you leaving?

TERESA

No. You want me to?

RAY

No. Do you want me to?

TERESA

You can do what you want!

RAY

What I want is for you to tell me why you couldn't sleep.

TERESA

Why are you up, anyway?

RAY

I heard you banging around out here and—

TERESA

How do you know what you heard? You were sleeping, weren't you? So you don't know what you heard.

RAY

Maybe I will go out.
He starts for the bedroom.

TERESA

Where?

RAY

Whata you care? You don't want me here.

TERESA

Do you wanna stay here?

RAY

What?

TERESA

Do you wanna stay here?

RAY

Yes.
He stops.

TERESA
So why go out?

RAY
Because you told me to, is why. That's why.

TERESA
I never did. What'd I say? I think the least you can do is tell me
what I said.
Facing him across the kitchen table.

RAY
Striding back to confront her across the table.
You think the least I can do is tell you what you said? Maybe you
should know what you said!

TERESA
I want the exact words—the exact words that you think I want you
to get out of here. What were they?

RAY
I don't know! You said them.
They are eyeball to eyeball, leaning on the table.

TERESA
And you heard them!

RAY
I know what I feel. That's what I know. And what I feel is—

TERESA
So this is about what you feel! Is that what this is about?

RAY
Some of it.

TERESA
Who cares what you feel, Ray? Who the hell cares?

RAY
I do. Sometimes.

TERESA
Like when? Like now? So what is it?

RAY
I ain't sure.

TERESA
Want me to tell you?

RAY
Do I want you to tell me what I feel?

TERESA
Yeah.

RAY
No!

TERESA
I will.

RAY
I don't want you to!

TERESA
Why?

RAY
Because how the hell would you know?
Turning, he heads for the bedroom again.

TERESA

Because it's not that hard, Ray. You're not some mystery figure after all, are you.

RAY

This stops him, and he comes back to the table.

I feel like—you wanna know what I feel like is somebody gave me a glass full of razor blades!

Sitting, demonstrating.

First they chopped them up, all these razor blades. They ground them up in this razor blade blender, different brands and different kinds, all these razor blades, until they were like this jagged foam, which they then put them in this liquid, maybe milk, and gave them to me to drink and I drank them.

TERESA

So who would do that? Me? Is that what you're implying?

RAY

I don't know. Would you?

TERESA

No. Because that's how I feel, too, you know. I don't feel so good either. Maybe you gimme some razor blade foam to drink, too?

RAY

No.

TERESA

I ain't so sure.

RAY

Why would you say that about me? What possible justification could you come up with in the name of such a thing?

TERESA

I got something.

RAY
Oh, you do, huh? What?

TERESA
You don't really want to know.

RAY
Unless I miss my guess, I'm asking.

TERESA
Because you forgot my birthday, you know?

RAY
I did?

TERESA
That's right.
Turning her back on him.

RAY
I did?
Very guilty.
Are you sure?

TERESA
Of course I'm sure. It's my birthday, isn't it?

RAY
When was it? Wait a minute, what day is today?

TERESA
It was yesterday.

RAY
It was yesterday?
He goes to her.
Oh, I just missed it barely. I'm sorry.

TERESA
It's okay.

RAY
We could still do something.
Taking her in his arms.

TERESA
We don't have to.

RAY
I'm really sorry. So that's what's bothering you.

TERESA
It's one of the things.

RAY
One of the things? It's one of the things bothering you? So there's other things?

TERESA
Yes. That's right. There's one more. One more thing.

RAY
Do you know what we can have? We can have a belated birthday dinner or some friends, okay?

TERESA
If you want.

RAY
I'd like to.

TERESA
It's up to you.

RAY
What's the other thing?

TERESA
You'll get mad.

RAY
No I won't.
He leans back, as if to see her from a distance.

TERESA
Yes you will. I think you will.

RAY
Test me.

TERESA
Whata you mean? How can I test you?

RAY
Just tell me.

TERESA
Then it won't be a test.

RAY
Sure it will.
Very reassuring, holding her close once again.

TERESA
No it won't, Ray. It'll be real.

RAY
No it won't.

TERESA
Okay, if you say so. I'll test you. I'm pregnant.

RAY
> *Stepping back, he looks at her.*

Whata you mean?

TERESA

I'm pregnant, Ray.

RAY

Since when?

TERESA

See.
> *She pulls a pregnancy test vial from her pocket.*

RAY

That's one of those things.

TERESA

Yeah.

RAY

It says you're pregnant?

TERESA

Because of the color.
> *She lays it on the table.*

RAY

How can you tell?
> *They bend over the vial to study it.*

TERESA

It's the color tells you. That's what I was doing, you know—why I was up. I was trying to see what the test said, because I was late and everything and I was trying to do it in secret, so you wouldn't see me, and then the test came out positive, I threw this glass, which I had in my hand, this glass of water I was drinking, and I

knew you heard it, because I heard you moving around right after, so I started pretending I was looking for something but I wasn't.

RAY

I see. And so when I asked you what you were looking for—

TERESA

I said I wasn't looking for anything!

RAY

Because you had no idea what you were looking for!

TERESA

Right! I had no idea, so I said I wasn't looking for anything!

RAY

You couldn't say you were looking for nothing!

TERESA

How could I say that?

RAY

I see, I get it. So Teresa, you threw something?

TERESA

Yeah. This glass of water which was in my hand.
Walking to pick up the glass.
And fortunately the glass when I threw it was plastic. Here it is.

RAY

Why did you throw it?

TERESA

C'mon, Ray. God. I'm just twenty-two years old, you know. I'm not very old and now I'm pregnant. I'm married and everything. So yeah, I'm worried. I worry about us. Don't you worry about us?

RAY

Oh, no.

He sits back at the kitchen table.

TERESA

You don't?

Sitting opposite him.

How can you not worry about us? Anybody in their right mind would worry about us, I think. Don't you ever?

RAY

Well, sometimes.

TERESA

That's what I mean. Because I worry we didn't get off to such a good start and everything. With the way, you know, things started out. I mean, me killing your dog and everything.

RAY

Ohh, c'mon. Don't worry about that.

TERESA

I do.

RAY

You didn't kill my dog.

TERESA

Well, not actually, no. But I was involved. I didn't mean to be, but I was.

RAY

I killed my dog. It was me.

TERESA

I just was mad.

RAY

I know.

TERESA

My feelings was hurt.

RAY

Teresa, listen to me on this score, because I don't want you to waste one more valuable second worryin' about all that happened then, okay. It was time for me to grow up is all. I mean, what was I doing hanging around with a stupid dog anyway? I was acting like a child, but I wasn't a child anymore. It was time for me to grow up. It was time for me to understand the way things really worked, and so I did that, and the dog died. I was immature and, you know, acting like a child way past any time that was within my rights—how long did I expect to keep doing that? You know, coming home and playin' with my stupid dog, like a baby, you know. Like some little baby.

> *Rising, he gets a bottle of whiskey and a glass from the shelves.*

I mean, how long did I think that was going to last? It hadda come to an end.

TERESA

And so you don't hold no grudge against me? Because I think you do sometimes.

RAY

No, no.

> *Pouring a drink.*

TERESA

Then how come your eyes are very angry? They're very angry.

RAY

No, they're not.

TERESA

God, you don't even know it.

RAY

Let's go back to bed.

TERESA

You don't even know it, Ray.

RAY

Who knows why anything happens, Teresa.
He drinks.

TERESA

That's what I'm saying. We're in terrible trouble here and we don't even know it. What about Joey? Do you hold a grudge against him?

RAY

No.

TERESA

He's my brother, you know?

RAY

Taking her by the arm, he heads for the bedroom.
Let's just go to bed. I'm tired.

TERESA

You're always tired, Ray. What's wrong with you? God!
The cordless wall phone rings and she pulls free of him.
Who could that be at this hour?

RAY

Don't answer it.

TERESA
Are you serious?

RAY
The hell with them.

TERESA
Don't we gotta answer it, Ray?

RAY
I don't wanna talk to them.

TERESA
But we do. It could be an emergency.

RAY
It's not.

TERESA
People don't call at three in the morning unless it's an emergency.
Grabbing the phone.
Hello?
*Ronnie, his cell phone to his ear, appears on the downstage
right corner, near the brick walls, around the corner from
the apartment door.*

RONNIE
Teresa, hello? This is Ronnie. Is Ray there?

TERESA
Oh, hi, Ronnie. Yeah, sure.
To Ray.
It's for you. It's Ronnie.

RAY
What's he want?

TERESA
I don't know.
Into phone.
Whata you want, Ronnie?

RONNIE
I wanna talk to Ray.

TERESA
He wants to talk to you.

RAY
Of course he wants to talk to me, he's callin' me up at three in the morning. But what does he want?

TERESA
Into the phone.
He wants to know what you want exactly, if you could tell me so—

RAY
Grabbing the phone.
Whata you want, Ronnie?

RONNIE
I wanna come by.

RAY
Why?

RONNIE
I'm real close by.

RAY
It's the middle of the night.

RONNIE
I know, but I'm real close.

RAY
How close?

RONNIE
Actually? I'm in your hallway.

RAY
You're in my hallway?

RONNIE
Yeah.

RAY
What are you doin' there?

RONNIE
You know, I come up the stairs, I'm in the hallway.

RAY
To Teresa.
He's in our hallway.
Back to the phone.
What the hell are you doing in our hallway, Ronnie?

TERESA
What's he want?

RAY
To Teresa.
I don't know what he wants. I know only that he's in the hallway.

RONNIE
I just need a minute.
*He walks around the corner of the brick wall to the door,
which puts him out of view.*
Could you let me in for a minute? I'm right outside your door.

The buzzer rings.
That's me.

TERESA
Is that him?
Moving to the door.

RAY
He says it is.

TERESA
She opens the door and there's Ronnie.
Wow, yeah, he is. Hello, Ronnie.

RONNIE
Stepping in.
Hi, Ray. Everybody's up, huh?

RAY
He hangs up the phone.
What's goin' on, Ronnie? Are you alone?

TERESA
You want a sandwich or something, Ronnie?

RAY
No, he don't want a sandwich.

TERESA
Maybe he could answer for himself.

RONNIE
I'm fine, Teresa, thank you.

TERESA
I'm kind of hungry, actually.

RAY

Then you eat the sandwich. Leave Ronnie out of it.

TERESA

How about you, Ray? You want a sandwich?

RAY

You can leave me out of it, too. You're the only one hungry here.

TERESA
Heading off to the kitchen.

Okay.

Ray's cell phone rings. And Ray, startled, looks at the phone lying on a kitchen shelf.

RONNIE

That's you, Ray.

RAY
Moving toward the phone.

You think I don't know that? I know that.

RONNIE

I'm just sayin' . . .

RAY

What?

RONNIE

Maybe you should skip it.

RAY
Opening his cell phone, seeing the readout.

Unknown person.

TERESA

Why shouldn't he answer, Ronnie?

RAY

Yeah, why the hell shouldn't I answer?

RONNIE

Maybe you don't wanna.

RAY

And maybe I do! I mean, it can't be you, can it, so how bad could it be?
Into the cell phone.
Yeah! Hello!
Lights up on Joey striding in downstage, talking on his cell phone.

JOEY

Hey, Ray. You got a minute? It's me, Joey.

RAY

Oh, Joey?

JOEY

Yeah.

RAY

Covering the phone, turning to Ronnie.
It's Joey.

RONNIE

What's he want?

RAY

I don't know—maybe I'll talk to him and find out.
Back into the phone.
Yeah?

JOEY

You got a minute?

RAY
Yeah, sure.

JOEY
How's Teresa?

RAY
You wanna talk to her?

JOEY
Actually, no. If the truth be told, it's you.

RAY
It's me what?

JOEY
Although it's not in fact you I wanna talk to in the long run. It's just you I gotta start with.

RAY
I see, you're gonna start with me but you wanna end with some-body else.

JOEY
Yeah. That friend of yours. I can't find him.

RAY
What friend? I don't know who you mean.

JOEY
Of course you do. You know very well you do. The guy he caused all our problems. Birnbaum.

RAY
That's who you're looking for?

JOEY
My uncle is looking for him.

RAY
He is? He's looking for Ronnie?

JOEY
That's right. Uncle Mal calls me up these days—he can't get enough of me—he says he don't know why, but he wants to see me. Well, it's—if you ask me—if anybody cares to hear my opinion—it's to break my balls. It's by rote now—he don't even have to think about it—he just does it, he can do it with one hand tied behind his back. So he's doin' that, you know. He's breaking my balls and do you know what? It's an accident, I don't know how or why anymore, but I let it slip about fucking Birnbaum, and Uncle Mal wants to see him, but I can't find him.

RAY
You let what slip about Birnbaum?
Ronnie is signaling to get something across to Ray.
What's that, Teresa?!
Then he lowers the phone, his hand over the mouthpiece.

RONNIE
Hushed, taking off his coat and sitting at the table.
Don't tell him I'm here, Ray. I don't wanna talk to him.

RAY
Don't worry, don't worry. I won't.
Joining Ronnie at the table, he returns to the phone.
You were sayin' what, Joey? You let what slip about Birnbaum?

JOEY
What I'm gonna tell you now, if you laugh I wanna leave no doubt, I will break your fucking teeth with a hammer one by one. That's how I will break them. With a hammer. One by one. You got that?

RAY
I guess.

JOEY
You guess. Don't you ever learn?

RAY
I'm tryin'.

JOEY
Well, good. But do you know what I guess? My guess is you are remedial.

RAY
You want me to hang up on you, Joey? Is that what you want?

JOEY
That would be a mistake, Ray! You don't want to make any more mistakes with me and my uncle. So listen to me. Just listen to me! I wouldn't believe this myself if I hadn't seen it with me own eyes and ears, but I was the witness, all right, and this goddamn Birnbaum—he does in fact—just as he claims he does—he has these psychic abilities. I saw them, personally.

RAY
Wait a minute, wait a minute. You're saying this about Ronnie?

JOEY
Yes. That's right. Birnbaum, he's—

RAY
You're talking about *Ronnie*?

RONNIE
Whispering.
He's sayin' what about me, Ray?

JOEY

You heard what I tol' you, didn't you!?

RAY

Ronnie Birnbaum! That's who you are—

JOEY

Hey, Ray! GET OVER IT! All right. It's just one of those things. You gotta adapt. But the point now is somehow I let this whole thing slip to Uncle Mal, and once he gets a sniff of it, you'd think the house was on fire, the way he's got me runnin' around, I'm grabbin' and reachin' and dumpin' out drawers, you know, to find the guy.

RAY

Why?

JOEY

Uncle Mal's got questions.

RAY

About what?

JOEY

I don't know. They're his questions. I mean, everything's a fucking mystery, right? As far as I am concerned, the prick is too mean to ever die, but he's sick and everything, you know. He wants to see what, if anything, Birnbaum knows about the unknown.

RAY

Right.

JOEY

You know. If he can shed some light.

          RAY
Well, sure, who wouldn't like that?

          JOEY
Right. So that's what Uncle Mal is looking for. But the first and most pressing mystery in my aggravating life is: where-is-this-jerkoff? So if—

          RAY
He's right here.

          JOEY
He's right where?

          RAY
Here. He's here with me.

          JOEY
He's there? He's right there with you?
          As Ronnie, his head in his hands, sinks in disbelief down to the table.

          RAY
Yeah.

          JOEY
What's he doin' there? He's there with you for what reason?

          RAY
I have no idea. He just showed up.

          JOEY
He showed up? Put him on. I wanna talk to him.

          RAY
          Covering the mouthpiece, he holds the phone out to Ronnie.
He wants to talk to you.

RONNIE

Ray, how could you do this to me? I asked you, Ray. I begged you.

RAY

I know.

JOEY

Pacing.

TELL HIM TO GET ON THE FUCKING PHONE, RAY! I'M SICK A THIS!

RONNIE

Why's he wanna talk to me? I don't wanna talk to him.

RAY

He says—do you know what he says? That you got psychic abilities.

RONNIE

That's what he says?

JOEY

PICK UP THE PHONE, YOU SONOFABITCH!

RAY

What the hell did you tell him, anyway?

RONNIE

Why? Whata you care?

RAY

Because you're here in my apartment in the middle of the night and this is what's going on, and if that ain't good enough reason, I don't need a goddamn reason! Why would you tell him that?

RONNIE

Because it's true.

RAY
Because it's true?

RONNIE
That's right.

RAY
Because it's true? So this is enough reason you tell people?

RONNIE
That's right.
Taking the phone, Ronnie covers the mouthpiece.
Why do you think I'm here?

RAY
You're askin' me? How the hell would I know?

RONNIE
Into the phone.
Hey, Joey. What's up?

JOEY
Birnbaum, that's you.

RONNIE
Yes, it is, Joey.

JOEY
How you doin'?

RONNIE
Okay. You?

JOEY
Whata stroke of luck, huh? You're at his house. I call there. I have no idea.

RONNIE

Hey, you know. Sometimes things work out. Right? Whata you want?

JOEY

You tell me.

RONNIE

I should tell you?

JOEY

Yeah.

RONNIE

I don't know what you want, Joey.

JOEY

Sure you do.

RONNIE

No, I don't.

JOEY

You're the fucking extraterrestrial, right, with all these superhero abilities, isn't that right?

RONNIE

Yeah, I guess, but I still don't know why you called me.

JOEY

I want you to meet me in the park. You're at Teresa and Ray's place, right?

RONNIE

What park?

JOEY
Take a guess, I'm thinking of it.

RONNIE
C'mon, Joey. I'm not a toy here. I'm not some stupid toy for you
to play with in this thing.

JOEY
Sure you are.

RONNIE
I don't think so.

JOEY
Where we met Uncle Mal. That park. That's the park I'm talking
about.

RONNIE
Oh. Why?

JOEY
Because it's convenient.

RONNIE
It's convenient to who, Joey?

JOEY
Listen. How quick can you be there?

RONNIE
You're talking about now? I was thinking in the morning, or
maybe tomorrow afternoon.

JOEY
No. I'm starting out now. I'm leaving right this second. I want you
to leave right this second, too. And answer your phone from now

on. You ain't been answerin' your phone. For the next foreseeable future, I am your sole preoccupation, so your phone rings, you answer, because it could be me!

RONNIE
Listen, Joey.

JOEY
Put Ray on!

RONNIE
Presenting the phone to Ray.
He wants to talk to you, Ray.

RAY
What for?

RONNIE
He didn't say.

RAY
Into the phone.
Yeah, Joey, it's me, Ray.

JOEY
Get him outa there. You see that he leaves right this minute.

RAY
Whata you telling me for? Tell him.

JOEY
I tol' him. Now I'm tellin' you. I tol' him his part, now I'm tellin' you your part. Just see that he does it. I don't wanna be kept waiting!
He hangs up and walks off.

> RAY
> *Closing the phone up.*

He wants you to get out of here.

> RONNIE

I know. Listen, Ray.
> *Getting up, he slips into his jacket.*

Are you listening to me, I want you to listen to me.
> *As Ray studies him.*

You gotta do it! There's something you don't wanna do, but you gotta. Okay?

> RAY

What?

> RONNIE

You gotta do it!
> *Heading for the door.*

> RAY

What are you talking about?

> RONNIE

I don't know.
> *He goes out the door.*

> RAY
> *Hurrying after Ronnie, but leaving the door open.*

You don't know what you're talking about, but you're telling me I—
> *Ray catches Ronnie in the hallway.*

What are you telling me?

> RONNIE

I only know the "you-gotta-do-it" part. That's all I know.

> RAY

Gotta do what?

Teresa returns, walking up to the table with a glass of milk and a plate containing a sandwich and chips. She looks out the open door.

TERESA
What are you guys talking about?

RAY
Tell her, Ronnie.

RONNIE
You tell her.

RAY
Grabbing Ronnie, Ray pushes him back into the apartment.
He's tellin' me I gotta do something, but he don't know what it is—I don't know what it is.

RONNIE
But you gotta do it!

RAY
He don't know, I don't know—we don't know.
He's crossing toward the bedroom.

TERESA
Is that right, Ronnie?

RONNIE
Apparently nobody knows.

RAY
But I gotta do it!
He goes into the bedroom.

                    RONNIE
                    Calling after him.
That's right!

                    TERESA
Geeze, Ronnie, how can you talk about something you don't know
what it is?

                    RONNIE
It ain't easy.
                    Starting out the door again.

                    TERESA
                    She holds up the sandwich to stop him.
You know I made you a sandwich in spite of what you said,
Ronnie.

                    RONNIE
I am in fact famished, Teresa. But could I take it with me, if you
don't mind?

                    TERESA
Sure. But you gotta drink the milk here. I need the glass.
                    She hands him the glass of milk and moves to the table.
I can wrap it up for you if you want. Geeze, Ronnie, why is Ray
being so mean to you?

                    RONNIE
Well, you know, I'm botherin' him.
                    He follows her to the table.
See, I got these psychic abilities, Teresa— You know—I don't like
them. I don't want them, but—

                    TERESA
Wow, Ronnie! How'd that happen?
                    *She pulls baggies from a drawer and starts packing his
                    sandwich and chips.*

RONNIE

I think it started in actuality when I was a kid.

TERESA

When you was a kid, Ronnie?

RONNIE

He crouches, his chin on the table, milk in hand.
Yeah, but I kept it a secret mostly.

TERESA

A little kid?
Ray, a shirt and trousers on, comes in, carrying shoes, zipping up his trousers. He stands behind Teresa, listening.

RONNIE

So I get like information sometimes I feel certain people should
have it. I mean like I come here tonight.
Bragging a bit, trying to impress Teresa.
I don't even know why, except I couldn't sleep. So I'm out on the
street. This way, that way. I have some coffee. Walking, walking. I
have some more coffee. I'm headed for the river. I got it in sight,
but I don't go to the river. I come over here and say, "Ray! You
gotta do it!"

RAY

Ronnie. Shut up.
To Teresa.
You wanna go to bed, Teresa. Ronnie's gotta go.

TERESA

She stands, suddenly scolding Ronnie.
Please hurry up and finish the milk, will you, Ronnie. I want to
clean up before I go back to bed and I'm exhausted!
*Ronnie starts to drink his milk, as Ray zeros in on him from
the other side.*

RAY

There's a lot of things I gotta do that I don't wanna do, Ronnie. One hell of a lot of them.

TERESA

RONNIE, I'M WAITING! CAN'T YOU SEE ME STANDING HERE?

RAY

Teresa was banging things around and I could hear her, so I gotta get up. I don't even wanna know what she's doin', but I gotta ask her, and I gotta listen to her. I mean a lota things *gotta* be done in these circumstances, goddamnit, Ronnie! What the hell are you talking about!

RONNIE

Finishing the milk, lowering the glass.

I feel like crying, Ray.

RAY

What? You oughta feel like crying, you're such an asshole.

RONNIE

Maybe she can help.

I feel like crying, Teresa.

TERESA

Are you gonna, Ronnie?

RONNIE

I don't know. Maybe.

TERESA

Did you tell him about the baby?

RAY

What baby?

TERESA
Me and Ray. We're having a baby.

RONNIE
Oh, I didn't know that.

TERESA
Why didn't you tell him?

RAY
It slipped my mind.

TERESA
We just found out.

RONNIE
Well, congratulations. Thank you for the milk.
He hands her the glass.
Here's the glass.

TERESA
Thank you.

RONNIE
That's very exciting for you, Teresa.

TERESA
Yes it is.
She heads toward the bedroom.
Well, goodnight.

RAY
Looking after her, he turns to Ronnie.
Do you know what I'm thinking? I'm thinking I done it already.

RONNIE
What?

RAY

The thing I don't wanna do, but I gotta.

RONNIE

That ain't the way it looks to me, Ray.

RAY

Ronnie! Why the fuck am I even listening to you about such stuff as you've been saying? Can you answer me that?

He grabs the whiskey bottle and glass from the shelf.

Personally, I have no idea. Because you wander around at night? This is your credentials?! You don't know where you're going. I should pay attention because you set out for one place but you end up in another. This is not a good enough qualification, Ronnie! If you were me, would you take one word you said seriously? I'm asking you! One word!

Ronnie, with his sandwich and chips in the baggie, rises and moves for the door.

And if one, which one? "DO IT! DO IT! GOTTA DO IT!" You know what, Ronnie?

RONNIE

What?

RAY

Good-bye, Ronnie.

RONNIE

Good-bye, Ray.

Ronnie goes. Ray sits at the table, facing the door and pouring a drink, as Teresa comes back.

TERESA

Wow. That was weird, huh?

RAY

What was?

TERESA
All that stuff he was saying.

RAY
Did you think so?

TERESA
Yeah. Didn't you?

RAY
Pouring another drink.
You're what's weird. That's what I think.

TERESA
You're not gonna get drunk, are you, Ray? Don't drink too much, okay?

RAY
Mocking her.
Okay.

TERESA
C'mon, honey, let's go to bed, okay. I feel funny. I feel scared.

RAY
Yeah? Do you?

TERESA
Gimme a hug, would you, okay? I feel— I want you to hold me, Ray.
As she tries to hug him from behind, he gets to his feet.

RAY
Getting to his feet.
No.

TERESA

Ray, honey, c'mon—you said you weren't going to drink too much. Isn't that what you said?

RAY

Yeah.

TERESA

Then what are you doing?

RAY

This isn't too much.
Pouring and drinking.
This is the right amount. How could it be too much?
Pouring a little more.
Every time I do it, it's perfect.

TERESA

Ray. Please, c'mon, okay?

RAY

No, no, watch.
Pouring more, then more, nearly filling the glass.
Well, that might be too much. But it's flawless drinking.
He takes a sip.
Flawless.
Another gulp.
Flawless. Perfection.
Gasping, he downs the rest as fast as he can and ends up shuddering, almost growling as he sets the glass on the table.
Ghaaaaahh. Ghaaaahh. Mind-boggling perfection.
He grabs the bottle from the table, his jacket from the back of the chair.

TERESA

You're making me sad, Ray. I feel sad.

RAY

Yeah?

As he moves for the door.

So cry.

He goes. Teresa stands watching. Music. Lights out. The kitchen unit is wheeled away, maybe fit into the wall, and a unit of tangled leaves, tree branches, and vines is brought on to fill the upstage middle of the set. A long park bench is brought on and placed before the tangled leaves and vines. In the shadows, Tommy Stones moves about, scattering leaves from a canvas bag all over the ground. As he goes, Joey comes in and sits on the bench, cell phone in hand as he finishes dialing and the music goes out. The sound of a cell phone is heard ringing once, then again.

RONNIE

From off.

Hello?

JOEY

Into phone.

Ronnie?

Ronnie steps into view downstage left. He has his cell phone up to his ear and he and Joey talk via the cell phones. Joey is seated on the bench, and the lights throw a greenish leaf pattern on both of them, as Ronnie mimes walking forward.

RONNIE

Yeah.

JOEY

Where are you, Ronnie?

RONNIE

I'm comin'.

JOEY

I don't see you. Where are you, Ronnie?

RONNIE

I don't see you either, Joey.

JOEY

I'm on the park bench, Ronnie. Where are you?

Just then a shadowy figure, THE PRIEST, enters upstage right, and Joey sees the figure, moving. The Priest strolls along, heading off behind the upstage unit of trees, vines, and branches.

RONNIE

I'm comin' into the park. I'm just comin' in.

JOEY

Rising, moving to get a better look at the departing figure.

Oh, yeah. There you are.

RONNIE

Where?

JOEY

Peering off upstage through the bushes.

Is that you?

RONNIE

Trudging along, facing out.

I think so.

JOEY

At the end of the walkway. It don't look like you.

RONNIE

Who do I look like?

JOEY
I don't know.

RONNIE
I think I'm me. As far as I know.

JOEY
C'mon back here. You're in the shadows.
Ronnie steps into the park, where he sees Joey, who peers off, his back to Ronnie.

RONNIE
Here I am.

JOEY
Startled, whirling.
There you are. That wasn't you.

RONNIE
Where?

JOEY
Looking once again through the bushes and up left where the figure went.
Over there.

RONNIE
No. I'm here. Was somebody over there?

JOEY
I thought so.

RONNIE
Who?
Sitting down on the bench, his baggie on his lap.

JOEY
I don't know.

RONNIE
You saw them, though.

JOEY
I thought they was you.

RONNIE
Did it look like me?
He takes out the sandwich, along with the chips.

JOEY
No.
He moves toward Ronnie.
But you was comin', I was talkin' to you, so I concluded it was you.

RONNIE
Even if it didn't look like me.

JOEY
It was a mistake.
Sitting down, he eyes the sandwich.

RONNIE
Lemme tell you—for future reference—if it don't look like me, it probably ain't.

JOEY
Whata you got there?

RONNIE
I'm starving, Joey.

JOEY
What kinda sandwich is that?

RONNIE
Bologna. Some mayonnaise. There's lettuce. It's my dinner. Teresa made it.

JOEY
Can I have a bite?

RONNIE
Joey, I'm starving. C'mon, have some mercy. I been runnin' around for hours now, goin' here, goin' there. I'm the river. Then I'm—you know, you phone me. Now look at me. Lemme eat it. Can I eat it?

JOEY
I just want a bite.

RONNIE
Please. Joey, I'm like a fucking gerbil, I'm a rodent in a pinball machine. I ain't had a second to myself. I'm gonna pass out.

JOEY
Just tear me off a corner, for crissake! Or can't you do that either?

RONNIE
Okay, okay.
Working to tear the sandwich in half.
How big a corner?

JOEY
Use your judgment. It's your sandwich.

RONNIE
Like that?
Offering a piece.
How's that?

JOEY

That's fine, you know.
Taking the offered chunk.
Jesus Christ, Ronnie, it's just a sandwich. Whatever you think.
Thank you.

RONNIE

You're welcome.
They each take a bite and sit there chewing.

RONNIE

I didn't mean to make such a fuss. I think I'm sleep deprived.

JOEY

You ain't slept?

RONNIE

Not in days.

JOEY

You should get some sleep.

RONNIE

I know.

JOEY

How's everything else?

RONNIE

Okay. You know. For the most part.
Suddenly worried.
Like what?

JOEY

Well, primarily, I was wondering how things are in your psychic
abilities realm. How's that?

RONNIE
It's exhausting, Joey. That's the truth.

JOEY
Busy, huh?

RONNIE
It's getting like Grand Central Station. I'm tellin' you, the spooks are working me overtime—I'm gonna need a switchboard if this keeps up.

JOEY
What's goin' on, do you suppose? Somethin' must be up.

RONNIE
I have no idea.
And then he remembers.
Oh. Did you know Ray and Teresa are having a baby?

JOEY
No. Really. Wow, that's amazing. When are they gonna find out?

RONNIE
Whata you mean?

JOEY
Are you gonna tell them?

RONNIE
They tol' me.

JOEY
Who?

RONNIE
Ray and Teresa.

JOEY
How do they know?

RONNIE
Well, they— One of those tests. You know, those kits, you buy them at the drugstore.

JOEY
Wait a minute, wait a minute! They tol' you this, that's what you're saying. This is like they tol' you this in so many words.

RONNIE
At the apartment.

JOEY
You were just there.

RONNIE
Right.

JOEY
And they spoke to you about this. They confided.

RONNIE
Right.

JOEY
It's not like from the other kind of knowledge—the other world, or whatever.

RONNIE
Oh. No.

JOEY
Like how you knew about Irene.

RONNIE
No, no.

JOEY
I thought that's what it was.

RONNIE
No, no.

JOEY
Can I ask you something? I wanna ask you somethin'.

RONNIE
What?

JOEY
How is Irene?

RONNIE
How is she?

JOEY
Yeah. I worry about her, you know. She fell a long ways. I've worried about her a lot of years. And, you know, I was wondering, does she know I didn't mean for her to fall? That I was sneaking to see her. I just wanted to see her.

RONNIE
I don't know if she knows that or not, Joey.

JOEY
She's probably mad at me if she don't.

RONNIE
Is this what you wanted, Joey? I mean, you got me here to ask me about Irene?

JOEY
Oh, no.

RONNIE
Then what?

JOEY
I just thought as long as we were sitting here, I might as well ask.
So you don't know anything more about her?

RONNIE
No. Not that I know of.

JOEY
She had these long fingers, these very little birdy bones in her fingers, and this pale skin—she was part Irish, and being that way,
you know, so—so—being so— What's the word I'm lookin' for?

RONNIE
I don't know.

JOEY
Sure you do. There's a word and she was like it. China is like it,
too. I don't mean the country, but the cups and saucers—and she
was pale-skinned and—
            Struggling mightily.
—like porcelain, and very—dainty—only that's not the word—so
when she fell—

RONNIE
Fragile.

JOEY
Right!
            Almost accusingly.
See, you did know.

RONNIE
Fragile.

JOEY
That's what she was. She was very fragile, and so it must have been awful when she hit.
He looks at the floor, as if she lies there.

RONNIE
Yeah.

JOEY
But you ain't heard nothing from her.

RONNIE
I don't think so, Joey.

JOEY
But could you keep your ears open? Could you do me that favor and keep your ears open?

RONNIE
Yeah. Okay.

JOEY
She might say something. You might hear something.
A sudden thud from offstage startles them, and they both whirl to look at the bushes, the tree limbs.

JOEY
What's that?
They both hurry up to the limbs and leaves and watch as a figure moves along behind them.

RONNIE
Somebody's coming.

JOEY

Look at that.

> *Ray emerges around the stage right corner of the bushes, carrying his bottle of whiskey.*

RAY

I knew I'd find you guys here.

> *Reeling, as if he must sit or fall, he flops down on the bench.*

RONNIE

Yeah, how?

JOEY

So maybe he's got it, too, Ronnie.

> *He pursues Ronnie, who moves close to Ray.*

Maybe he's extrasensory, and that's how he knew, so you ain't so special as you think. How'd you feel about that?

RAY

> *Toasting Ronnie with his bottle.*

This better be what I "gotta do it," Ronnie, because it's what I'm gonna do!

> *Behind Joey and Ray, who are both facing Ronnie, The Priest has entered. He stands in the shadows near the edge of the bushes, leaves, branches, reading his Breviary. Looking past Joey and Ray, Ronnie is the only one who sees The Priest.*

JOEY

Or maybe somebody told him! Maybe somebody's a blabbermouth!

RONNIE

> *Whispering.*

There's a priest.

JOEY
What?

RAY
What?

RONNIE
With an urgent, yet secretive gesture.
Look at that.
Joey and Ray turn and look.

JOEY
What's he doin' here? Do you know him?

RONNIE
Maybe it was him you saw before, Joey. He don't look like me.
Taking note of them, The Priest steps closer.

PRIEST
Hello, boys.

RONNIE
Hello, Father.

PRIEST
Pleasant night, isn't it, boys?

RAY
Very nice.

JOEY
You're up awful late, ain't you, Father?

PRIEST
Early, my son. It's morning for me. Early bird catches the worm.
It's a lovely hour, isn't it?

JOEY
Yeah. Lovely.

RONNIE
Very pleasant, Father.
The Priest strolls off down right and they all three peer after him. Joey even moves after The Priest.

RAY
What's he doin'?

RONNIE
Some of them like to walk around when they say their morning office. Ain't you ever seen that?

RAY
Yeah. Sure.
He flops back, lying down on the bench.

JOEY
I didn't recognize him, did you? Maybe he's from a different parish.

RAY
Like you're keeping a close watch who is the pastor and who is the assistant pastor. You're such a devoted member of the flock, Joey, I had no idea.

JOEY
All I said is I ain't seen him.

RONNIE
Approaching Joey.
So, Joey, I'm wondering, if you didn't bring me here to ask me about Irene, why did you bring me here?

RAY
You ain't told him yet?

RONNIE
Tol' me what?
Behind them, from up left, Tommy Stones wheels Uncle Malvolio on.

UNCLE MALVOLIO
Tommy, look who's over here waitin' for us. It's Ronnie Birnbaum. Hello, Ronnie Birnbaum.
They all look as Tommy Stones parks the wheelchair left of the bench and Joey shoves Ronnie toward Uncle Malvolio.

JOEY
My uncle Mal has some questions for you.

TOMMY STONES
We meet again.

UNCLE MALVOLIO
And my nephew-in-law Ray. Ray Matz. He's here, too.

TOMMY STONES
I see him.

UNCLE MALVOLIO
Hello, Ray.

JOEY
Hello, Uncle Mal.

UNCLE MALVOLIO
Joey, you did good.

JOEY
It wasn't easy.

UNCLE MALVOLIO
Who cares?

JOEY
Ray's got some news, too, Uncle Mal.
To Ray.
Go on, Ray, tell him. You don't, I will.
Annoyed, Ray rises, shoving past Joey.

UNCLE MALVOLIO
Tell me what?

JOEY
I'm gonna be an uncle, too, Uncle Mal. Teresa and Ray are having
a baby.

UNCLE MALVOLIO
Is that a fact, Ray?

RAY
That's what she says.
Ray, with his bottle, leans against the wall.

UNCLE MALVOLIO
You know what? Guess what? There's no stopping it. So, Birnbaum.
*As Uncle Malvolio turns his attention to Ronnie, Joey
pushes Ronnie down on the bench.*
Rumor has it you talk to the dead. As you might guess, I find that
interesting.

RONNIE
Excuse me— What?

JOEY
He sits down on the other side of Ronnie.
You know you talk to the dead, Ronnie.

UNCLE MALVOLIO
This is what he tells me. Is he wrong? Because I got these matters, these issues—who doesn't? It won't be long, I'll be a ghost myself. But in the meantime, I figure talking to the dead might gimme an advantage.

RONNIE
To Joey.
You tol' him?

UNCLE MALVOLIO
The cat is outa the bag. I'm looking for some outside help. I wanna talk to the dead, too.

RONNIE
I don't know who I talk to, and it's more like they talk to me.

UNCLE MALVOLIO
Hey. Whatever. Whatsay we cut the shit, the clock is ticking. You wanna help me or not?

RONNIE
Sure, sure. I'm just saying, half the time, I don't know what I'm doin'.

UNCLE MALVOLIO
And the other half you're big time. So maybe we'll get lucky.

RAY
Dropping the bottle, puking.
Ahgggghhhhhh!!

UNCLE MALVOLIO

Oh, lookee him—he's gonna have green chunky stuff all over his shoes. Get him off in the bushes, at least, Joey.

Joey fastidiously maneuvers Ray up near the bushes.

UNCLE MALVOLIO

Should we have to witness him upchucking Burger King into his trouser cuffs, Birnbaum? I don't think so.

He watches Ray flop around on the ground.

Such a pathetic sight, and yet he makes me smile. Tommy, you got thirty bucks, go to the corner, the liquor store, get Ray here another bottle. I don't want him to run out.

RAY

Crawling back downstage.

Grrrhhhhgggghhhhhhhh. Graaaggghhhhhhhhhh.

UNCLE MALVOLIO

What's that, Ray?

RAY

He gestures at Uncle Malvolio.

Grraggggghhhhhhhh.

UNCLE MALVOLIO

You got nothin' to worry about. Tommy's gonna get you another bottle and maybe a nipple. Would you like a nipple?

RAY

Fuggg youuu!

Uncle Malvolio flashes with anger, and Tommy steps, threateningly, toward Ray.

UNCLE MALVOLIO

Tommy! Go on like I tol' you.

TOMMY STONES
You sure you'll be all right, Mal?

UNCLE MALVOLIO
Hey, it's ten steps over, ten steps back.
> *Tommy Stones starts off. Uncle Mal, with a darkened*
> *mood, wheels toward Ray.*
I'm gonna have some fun. Guess what, Ray? I think it's time some-body let you in on the joke. We was playing with you, you know. It was a setup. You was Saturday morning cartoons with your fuck-ing pet. But nobody was going to shoot you over the snit Teresa was in. You listening to me?

RAY
Yeah.
> *Kneeling, he looks up.*

UNCLE MALVOLIO
So whata you think?

RAY
> *Trying to focus.*
About what?

JOEY
We was just playin' with you.

UNCLE MALVOLIO
See. Joey knew. We all knew. And you knew, too. Admit it, Ray. You knew most of all, didn't you.

RAY
Knew what?

UNCLE MALVOLIO
That we wasn't really gonna shoot you.

RAY

Cause you said you was, you know. So why'd you do that?

UNCLE MALVOLIO

Because we were trying to scare you!

JOEY

We was scarin' you, Ray.

UNCLE MALVOLIO

Havin' some fun at your expense, you know—puttin' an extra nail into your soul.

RAY

But you weren't gonna shoot me?

UNCLE MALVOLIO

NO! HOW MANY TIMES DO I HAVE TO TELL YOU?!

RAY

No matter what?
 Wobbling, looking for Ronnie.
Is that right, Ronnie? Did you know that?

RONNIE

No.

RAY

 Facing Uncle Malvolio.
Then why'd I let you shoot my dog?

UNCLE MALVOLIO

Because you're gutless. That's what you gotta know. All you hadda do is take a chance for him. You had any real balls, he could still be around, scratchin' fleas and lickin' his asshole.

RAY

Ohhhh, nooo. No, no. No, no.

Ray collapses to the ground, where he sits, glaring at Uncle Malvolio.

UNCLE MALVOLIO

That's right! Fuck you! But enough with the fun and games.

Wheeling back, he settles on the stage right side of Ronnie on the bench.

So Birnbaum, let's get down to brass tacks. Which is you and me. Because in spite of the fact that I'm Chemo, I'm radioactive— I got mastasized into the bones so I feel like I have fallen off some tall building and every second, I'm landing. I'm landing, that's all I do. But in spite of that, I'm still breathing and because of that there are these guys who are so fucking impatient, they can't wait for nature to take its course—so as a result, someone has put a contract out on me. Can you believe it? So I'm wondering: Who is planning to kill me? I am putting my money on the dead can tip me off, and then I will be able to turn the tables on these assholes who are planning to kill me one last time and I will kill them. So this is where you come in. You with me so far, Birnbaum?

RONNIE

I think so.

UNCLE MALVOLIO

What we gotta do is get a name for who is plotting against me. You can understand my curiosity, right?

RONNIE

Sure, sure.

UNCLE MALVOLIO

So let's get started.

RONNIE

But I just get stuff, you know. It comes to me—half the time I don't even know who it's for even.

Tommy saunters in with a new bottle of bourbon.

UNCLE MALVOLIO

Hey, Ray! Wake up! Give him a kick, Tommy.

Tommy pokes Ray, who stirs, and Tommy sticks the bottle into Ray's hands.

He's got your bottle, Ray! That's right, there you go.

Tommy moves back close to Uncle Malvolio.

Okay, so the dipso here is content. Now what? How do we roll this fucking truck?

RONNIE

I don't know if I can do this or not.

UNCLE MALVOLIO

Birnbaum, you're whinin'. Stop it! Be a pro.

TOMMY STONES

You want us to help? We'll help.

JOEY

Sitting down next to Ronnie.

Just tell us what to do. We don't know what to do.

RONNIE

Sometimes . . . I close my eyes, and if I close my eyes and breathe real deep it helps.

UNCLE MALVOLIO

So do it.

RONNIE

Okay, okay—and I'm thinking—maybe if we all, if everybody—I don't know what I'm talking about here for sure, but if we all close

our eyes and breathe deep. Deeper than usual. Way deeper than usual. And we just keep doing it, and keep our eyes closed, it might help.

UNCLE MALVOLIO
Wait a minute, you want us all sittin' here with our eyes closed? No, no, we need a lookout. I say Tommy stays alert. Right, Tommy?

TOMMY STONES
Sure, sure, that's smart.

UNCLE MALVOLIO
You can do the breathing part. But other than that, you are a watchdog. I don't want this guy, whoever he is, comin' up on me, I'm sittin' here like a fucking sunbather.

TOMMY STONES
Right.

UNCLE MALVOLIO
So we're all breathing, we're all sittin', we're real quiet—that's the plan. You had success along these lines, right, Birnbaum?

RONNIE
What you gotta understand is whatever comes into my head has to come outa my mouth, because it might be the clue you're looking for. Okay?

UNCLE MALVOLIO
You come up with it, I won't miss it.

RONNIE
Okay.

Closing his eyes, Ronnie breathes deeply, once, then again. After a big breath, his head bows forward.

UNCLE MALVOLIO

There he goes. Okay, Joey, you next.

Joey, doing his best to imitate Ronnie, takes a breath, and then with a breath like a man about to dive underwater, he bows forward.

JOEY

Here I go.

Uncle Malvolio breathes in and out, then shuts his eyes. Ray, downstage right, sags and falls sideways. Tommy Stones, standing behind the bench on guard duty, starts taking in sharp breaths like a man lifting weights. This goes on for a beat or two.

UNCLE MALVOLIO

Whispering.

Tommy?

TOMMY STONES

Yes, Mal?

UNCLE MALVOLIO

You okay?

TOMMY STONES

Hushed.

Yeah. Everything's quiet.

Ronnie and Joey each take a breath and let it out.

Except I'm gettin' the creeps.

A wind starts to blow over them.

UNCLE MALVOLIO

Good. That's good.

JOEY

You feel that wind coming up?

TOMMY STONES

Yeah. But is it the wind or maybe the onset of these whirling, you know, souls?

UNCLE MALVOLIO

Shhhhhhhhhhh. Let's hope it's the dead tiptoeing the fuck up.
Uncle Malvolio takes a breath, closes his eyes, and Ronnie's head rises, facing out, eyes opening slowly.

RONNIE

Long ago in a time when small things were important, men searched for a safe way to protect themselves from the elements. One such way was to stand all of mankind under the tree of life. Each protected in his own way by a single leaf on the tree.
His head lowers, and he's out again.

TOMMY STONES

What?

RONNIE

As his head comes back up.
When time passed and the tree of life, after all was done, had served its purpose, the leaves yellowed and dropped, leaving each man whose leaf dropped without protection. Such things were always in accord with the universe.

UNCLE MALVOLIO

I feel like I'm trying to read a fuckin' book.

RONNIE

Blue and red and green and gold—or cold— No, no. *Gold. Gold sparrows* are felt deep in the soul.

TOMMY STONES

"Gold sparrows"? You're saying, "Gold sparrows in the soul"?

RONNIE
"Sparrows"—yeah

TOMMY STONES
What the hell is that?

JOEY
Scolding Tommy.
He's tryin' to figure it out.

TOMMY STONES
But "sparrows"—what's he talking about?

RONNIE
More or less free of the trance.
This is a lot of pressure, you guys. I mean, maybe we should quit, because I— No! No! It's sorrows. Cold sorrows. Cold sorrows.

TOMMY STONES
There. See, Joey, I knew it couldn't be "sparrows."

RONNIE
Sorrows. Cold, cold sorrows felt deep in the soul. Joy is silver, tears are green. You will know just what I mean. The heart is purple, the soul is blue, look into deeply, what color are you?

TOMMY STONES
What?

RONNIE
What color are you?

TOMMY STONES
Who?

RONNIE
You!

UNCLE MALVOLIO
ALL RIGHT, ALL RIGHT! EVERYBODY GRAB THEIR
DICK! This is some numbnuts of a ghost Birnbaum has brought
us. You hear me, Birnbaum?! Who is this silly hairball you have
latched on to?!

RONNIE
Dead Sammy.

UNCLE MALVOLIO
Dead Sammy? Now I gotta hear from that bum?

RONNIE
He says he knew about you.

UNCLE MALVOLIO
So then, if he knew about me, why is he "Dead Sammy"?

RONNIE
Wait a minute, wait a minute. I got somethin' else.

UNCLE MALVOLIO
What?

TOMMY STONES
What?

RONNIE
It sounds like barking. It's barking.

JOEY
Barking?

RONNIE
Barking, you know. I got some barking.

JOEY
What kind of barking?

TOMMY STONES
Is there howling, too, or just barking?

RONNIE
Lots of barking, a little howling.

UNCLE MALVOLIO
NO, NO, NO! ENOUGH WITH THIS LIMP DICK BULLSHIT!
I think these souls you got here, Birnbaum, they are goofballs.
They are a bunch of clowns! I wanna request something. You pass
it along.

RONNIE
I'll try.

UNCLE MALVOLIO
Just do it. What you need to hook me up with is some darker elements. Some black, shadowy forces. You know. Evil. Somethin' to
be on my side.

RONNIE
Are you sure?

UNCLE MALVOLIO
I want you to bring a tortured, tormented soul right here in front
of me to talk to me right now!
 Ronnie shuts his eyes, starts breathing hard and fast,
 and Joey and Tommy Stones and Uncle Malvolio do
 the same, as Ray, slumped downstage right, slowly sits
 up, arms extended like a sleepwalker, yet aimed directly
 at Uncle Malvolio.

RAY
Hee Wagnaab! Normee! Normee!

It's as if he's putting a curse on Uncle Malvolio.
MANGODINGPOOF!

UNCLE MALVOLIO
What the hell's his problem now? He's messin' the whole thing up!
Shut him up!
> *Tommy and Joey storm over to Ray, kicking him.*

JOEY
Shut up, Ray!

TOMMY STONES
> *Overlapping.*
Shut up!
> *Joey and Tommy chase and kick Ray up near the wall until*
> *Ronnie starts to speak, loudly, in a kind of triumph.*

RONNIE
Your fears are realistic in your mind but not in reality.
> *Joey and Tommy Stones hurry back to their positions at the*
> *benches.*
Your paranoia is extreme only because of futuristic stances your
soul will take. There will be no harm to befall you. You are safe in
the presence of the unhunted.

UNCLE MALVOLIO
> *Grabbing Ronnie's arm.*
I'm safe? You're tellin' me I'm safe!

RONNIE
No. That was—that one was for Ray.
> *They all look at Ray crawling around in the corner.*

UNCLE MALVOLIO
Ray? Who gives a fuck about him? So Ray's safe? He don't look
safe. How can you say he's safe? He's groveling and puking.

RONNIE

I guess maybe he's done it.
Receiving a correction from the air.
No, no, they say he's gonna do it.

UNCLE MALVOLIO

He's gonna do what?

RONNIE

The thing he don't wanna do.

UNCLE MALVOLIO

WHAT ABOUT ME, FOR CRISSAKE? WHAT'S A PERSON
GOTTA DO TO GET A CHANCE IN THE GODDAMN
LIMELIGHT AROUND HERE?
*Ronnie shuts his eyes and plunges into deep loud breathing,
and the others follow suit, as if to force the spirit world to
give Uncle Malvolio his answer. So they are all distracted,
breathing loudly, as The Priest walks into their midst.*

PRIEST

Well, boys. Still at it, I see.
They just about jump out of their skins.

JOEY

Hello, Father.

UNCLE MALVOLIO

Hey, Father, you shouldn't just sneak up on people like that.
*As The Priest moves around the bench, Ray lunges,
grabbing The Priest's leg.*

RAY

Please, Father. Please.

PRIEST

What is it? What's he doing?

RAY
I betrayed him. I betrayed my friend.

PRIEST
What's wrong with him? Is he drunk?

RAY
I'm in trouble.

PRIEST
I'll tell you one thing, if you don't let go of my leg, you're going to find out what real trouble is!

RAY
I want your blessing. You gotta hear my confession, okay?

UNCLE MALVOLIO
Hey, Ray— SHUT UP!!

PRIEST
I'm sorry, but are you saying you want to go to confession right here?

RAY
Right here, right now.

PRIEST
But is that really such a good idea?

RAY
I'm afraid I'm gonna die. With every breath. With every breath I'm afraid I'm gonna die.

PRIEST
I see. Well.

RAY

It's stupid I know, but I gotta do it. I had him since he was a pup.
Can you gimme some penance?

UNCLE MALVOLIO

Father, I'm warning you—get this thing onto the fast track!

PRIEST
Bending down to Ray.
Who was a pup?

RAY

My frien'.

PRIEST

I assume you're speaking in a metaphorical sense, and your friend
was—

RAY

I'm speaking in the sense of a dog. He was a dog.

PRIEST

So this is a real dog?

RAY

He was very very real. And he never once did a mean thing to me.
Not once in six years.

PRIEST

I see. He was good.

RAY

He threatened to bite me once when I was pullin' this chicken bone
away from him, but he felt terrible about growling. You could—
And he did bite the UPS man, he hated the UPS man. I have no
idea why, and bit him, but—

UNCLE MALVOLIO
Father! Jump-start this motherfucker before I lose my temper!

RAY
He folds his hands to pray.
Oh my God I am heartily sorry for all my sins, but most of all, I'm sorry. I'm very, very . . . I just wanted to live, you know?
Sagging.
What's my penance?

PRIEST
Say four Our Fathers and twelve Hail Marys.

RAY
Okay . . . okay . . . In the name of the Father and of the Son and of the Holy Ghost . . .
He topples over and lays there out cold, breathing heavily.

UNCLE MALVOLIO
Whata bum. Poor Teresa.

PRIEST
Well, it's funny how these things work out, isn't it?
The Priest stands, looking down at Ray.

UNCLE MALVOLIO
So this is your idea of it worked out?

PRIEST
Fortuitous that I happened along is what I mean. He's feeling so frightened and guilty. And he's right, of course, to fear death, because it could just snatch him away at any second. Each breath could be his last. Fascinating, isn't it, the way they come one after the other, each one that isn't final bringing him closer to the one that will be.

UNCLE MALVOLIO
Hey, Father, you got a pretty ghoulish point of view on this thing here.

PRIEST
God's will and all that.

UNCLE MALVOLIO
You're a very macabre guy.

PRIEST
Well, death is man's best friend after all, opening the door on the pathway to God.

TOMMY STONES
He loves this shit.

UNCLE MALVOLIO
You base this opinion on you got some experience with this door? You been down this pathway?

PRIEST
No, no. Of course not. I base it on faith.

UNCLE MALVOLIO
Which is what?

PRIEST
Well, it's just a matter of faith.
Moving toward Uncle Malvolio.

TOMMY STONES
Which is what?

PRIEST
Well, which is my knowledge of what I have never experienced. What I have no need to experience.

Standing uncomfortably close to Uncle Malvolio.
Anyone else?

UNCLE MALVOLIO
For what?

PRIEST
Confession.

RONNIE
I don't think so, Father.

TOMMY STONES
Maybe later.

JOEY
Yeah. Maybe later.

PRIEST
Just remember, I have a seven a.m. Mass to say. So I'll be leaving
shortly.
*As The Priest goes, Uncle Malvolio follows a short way. He
stares after The Priest.*

UNCLE MALVOLIO
We'll keep that in mind.
*Joey and Tommy Stones join Uncle Malvolio, all looking
into the wake of The Priest.*

RONNIE
Who's Margot?

JOEY
What?

RONNIE
Who's Margot?

> ### UNCLE MALVOLIO
> Margot? Margot? What the fuck you talking about now?

> ### RONNIE
> Anybody know a Margot?

> ### TOMMY STONES
> Margot who?

> ### RONNIE
> I tol' you, "Margot" is all I got.

> ### TOMMY STONES
> You didn't tell us.

> ### RONNIE
> *Searching, working.*
> Margot. Margot. Margot. Margot.

> ### JOEY
> This is a spook you're talking about?

> ### RONNIE
> Yeah.

> ### TOMMY STONES
> This is a spook of the name of Margot?

> ### RONNIE
> Yeah.

> ### TOMMY STONES
> I don't.

> ### JOEY
> I don't. Not that I remember. What about you, Uncle Mal?

UNCLE MALVOLIO

No.

RONNIE

But it is.

UNCLE MALVOLIO

No.

RONNIE

But it is. It's you she wants. It's you she's looking for you. And she's big. Oh, boy, is she big. This is a big, big woman—and she's givin' you a bath. You're in a tub, a little tub and your belly is all wet and soapy, and her hands are patting you and rubbing you. She's smiling down at you. Her eyes are the color of your eyes. You're smiling up at her. Your eyes are shiny and your belly is shiny—and your skin smells like oats, fresh oats. And she smells like flowers. Daffodils. You're laughing, it's a bubbly gurgley blub blub little—

UNCLE MALVOLIO

WHO THE FUCK CARES?!! THIS SHAM IS OVER! I'M SHUTTING THIS JERKOFF OPERATION DOWN!

JOEY

Should we go, Uncle Mal?

UNCLE MALVOLIO

I don't care what you do. You bring me this fucking moron, Joey! You vouch for him. You recommend him. I should shoot the both of you!

JOEY

Starting to back away.

Come on, Ronnie.

> **TOMMY STONES**
>
> You're smart enough to know when this kind of thing has gone too far, Joey!
>
> > *Joey grabs at Ronnie, who just sits there, looking at Uncle Malvolio.*
>
> **JOEY**
>
> Ronnie, we gotta go!
>
> **UNCLE MALVOLIO**
>
> > *He rises from the wheelchair in a towering rage.*
>
> Shoot 'em. Tommy! Shoot the cocksuckers if they ain't outa my sight in ten motherfucking seconds!
>
> **TOMMY STONES**
>
> Get out of here, Joey!
>
> > *He waves his gun as a threat.*
>
> GODDAMNIT!!
>
> > *Joey pushes Ronnie off upstage left with Tommy right behind them.*
>
> **UNCLE MALVOLIO**
>
> > *Staggering up to Tommy.*
>
> Gimme the fucking gun, Tommy!
>
> > *Uncle Malvolio rips the gun from Tommy Stones's hand and stands looking off.*
>
> **JOEY**
>
> > *From off.*
>
> We're going, Uncle Mal!
>
> > *Uncle Malvolio stands trembling and looking after Joey and Ronnie.*
>
> **UNCLE MALVOLIO**
>
> Who does that smart mouth think he is?

TOMMY STONES
I don't know.

UNCLE MALVOLIO
Does he think he can say all that and just walk away?

TOMMY STONES
I have no idea, Mal. It takes all kinds.

UNCLE MALVOLIO
Callin' me a baby—what's he thinkin' about?
Staggering back, he flops down on the bench.
What a jerkoff. So I was a big shiny baby once. So what? So the fuck what? Who wasn't? And now I'm this—this hunk of leftover pizza, I been in the basement too long. They left me down there. They took me down to work on the plumbing, I was gonna be a snack. Then they forgot about me. They come up. They forgot about me in the basement. So here I am. So what?
Looking around.
Listen. Go find that priest for me.

TOMMY STONES
Yeah?

UNCLE MALVOLIO
Yeah. See if he's still around.

TOMMY STONES
You sure?

UNCLE MALVOLIO
Go on.
Gesturing.
He went off that way.

TOMMY STONES
I'll be right back.

Tommy Stones goes, leaving Uncle Malvolio alone on the bench. He sticks the gun under his sweater, holding it there, and waits, as The Priest enters from behind him. Startled, Uncle Malvolio begins to rise, almost pulling the gun out until he sees who it is.

UNCLE MALVOLIO
You got a light step there, Father.

PRIEST
My path back to the rectory takes me back this way.

UNCLE MALVOLIO
I just sent my guy to look for you.

PRIEST
Really?

UNCLE MALVOLIO
I wanted him to bring you where I could see you.

PRIEST
And here I am. Do you suppose we're once again mixed up in the mysterious workings of fate?

UNCLE MALVOLIO
This is what concerns me. How the hell would I know?

PRIEST
Glancing at his watch.
I'm running a little late.

UNCLE MALVOLIO
So what I want is for you to hear my confession, if you got the balls for it. Do you think you do?

PRIEST
I think I probably do.

UNCLE MALVOLIO
Good. Now according to my understanding, it's the letter of the law that as long as I lay the whole thing out to you in person, I can get away with an imperfect act of contrition. Is that correct?

PRIEST
Well, yes. In a manner of speaking.

UNCLE MALVOLIO
Well, let's be in that manner, because I think I can manage imperfect.
The Priest settles down on the bench beside Uncle Malvolio.

PRIEST
And how long has it been since your last confession?

UNCLE MALVOLIO
Who remembers.

PRIEST
He holds his Breviary near his head, creating the semblance of a partition between them.
So it's been a long time, we'll say.

UNCLE MALVOLIO
Yeah. Let's say that.

PRIEST
And what is it you wish to confess, my son?

UNCLE MALVOLIO
Bless me, Father, I have sinned. I've sinned, and sinned, and sinned, and sinned and—

Ronnie hurries in from down right. He carries a small brown paper bag, and he halts, seeing Uncle Malvolio stand to face him.

UNCLE MALVOLIO
Whata you want?

RONNIE
I hadda come back.

UNCLE MALVOLIO
What for? You ain't brought her with you. That fuckin' Margot, you ain't brought my mother back, I hope.

RONNIE
No.

UNCLE MALVOLIO
You're sure.

RONNIE
No. She's gone.

UNCLE MALVOLIO
So what are you doin' then? Because you are on dangerous ground you come here like this, you interrupt me at such a moment when—

PRIEST
Indignantly standing up.
Excuse me, but are we going to continue, or not?

UNCLE MALVOLIO
Hang on to your shorts there, Father. This guy is—

PRIEST
I'm afraid I can't wait. We're in the midst of a sacrament.

RONNIE
But I have very important information.

PRIEST
I don't care. He needs to do this.
He sits back down.
I need a little more than what you have so far provided. You can't
just say "sinned and sinned" and call it a confession.

UNCLE MALVOLIO
Returning to the bench.
Whata you want, details? Okay, sure. My sin, biggest sin, my biggest
sin—I don't regret one thing I ever did—my only regret is what I am.
That once I was a brand-new baby with big eyes and rosy cheeks and
now I'm this puddle of crap and pus in piss-stinking pajamas!

PRIEST
But that's not a sin.

UNCLE MALVOLIO
Bullshit!
*Leaping up, the gun comes out, like it's part of his hand as
he staggers toward where Ray lays.*
Once I was a sweet-smelling baby, and now look at me. So that's
my sin, that's my confession. Fuck you, are you gonna give me ab-
solution?
He looks down at Ray.
You see this bum at my feet—this bum and my niece Teresa are
having a baby. So the whole fucking mess starts all over again!
To The Priest.
Where's my absolution?

PRIEST
But you're not sorry for your sins.

UNCLE MALVOLIO
I don't have to be. We negotiated—we made a deal.

PRIEST
We don't make deals.

RONNIE
Jumping up.
I gotta interrupt! I got something to tell you!

UNCLE MALVOLIO
Gesturing at Ronnie with the gun.
Shut up! You fucking moron! I'm trying to talk to Father Whatsiss here!

PRIEST
Excuse me, but why are you threatening him? Stop waving that gun around! Put that gun down!

UNCLE MALVOLIO
WHAT?!

PRIEST
Look at you! You're continuing to sin right in front of me!

UNCLE MALVOLIO
WHO THE HELL ASKED YOU?! SHUT UP! FUCK YOU!
Pointing the gun directly at The Priest's head.
JUST GIMME MY GODDAMN ABSOLUTION!

PRIEST
No, no, I can't when you talk this way.
He backs away.
I can't give you absolution.

UNCLE MALVOLIO
Where you goin'?
Pursuing several steps after The Priest.

PRIEST
I'm sorry. I can't. I'm sorry.
He goes.

UNCLE MALVOLIO
You're sorry! Who the hell cares you're sorry!?
Wheeling to face Ronnie.
Did you see that, Birnbaum?! I ask him, we negotiate—you're my
witness—it's fair and square.
Staggering back, he sits in his wheelchair.
All of a sudden, he walks out on me. I shoulda known he'd give
me nothing, except he's a joke, except he's a ball-less prick in a
dress! He had nothin' for me anyway, did he, Birnbaum. But you
got somethin' for me, right? That's why you come back.

RONNIE
Yeah.

UNCLE MALVOLIO
Good. Good. So it's you and me and the spooks. I'll do the breathing again, okay.

RONNIE
You don't have to.

UNCLE MALVOLIO
No, no. I wanna.
*As Ronnie sits on the edge of the bench nearest the wheel-
chair, he places the paper bag under the bench, while Uncle
Malvolio takes in one big breath, then exhales and looks
eagerly to Ronnie.*

UNCLE MALVOLIO
So whata you got for me?

RONNIE
It's your turn.

UNCLE MALVOLIO
Whata you mean?

RONNIE
It's your turn.

UNCLE MALVOLIO
That's what they're sayin'? It's my turn?

RONNIE
Yeah.

UNCLE MALVOLIO
Okay. Okay.
Leaning in.
It's my turn for what?

RONNIE
To be the dog.

UNCLE MALVOLIO
To be the dog?

RONNIE
With a growing realization of dread.
It's your turn to . . . be the dog.
Rising, retreating from Uncle Malvolio.
It's your turn to be the—

UNCLE MALVOLIO
THIS DOG AGAIN!! WHAT'S HIS FUCKING PROBLEM?
Suddenly, as if shot, gasping, his chest shutting down.
Owwwww! Owwwww!
He clutches his chest.
Birnbaum! BIRNBAUM!

RONNIE
Yeah.

UNCLE MALVOLIO
Ahhhhhhhh, shit. What is this? What . . . the . . . hell—OWWW,
OWWW—is this? For crissake, gimme a hand here!

RONNIE
Edging closer.
What?

UNCLE MALVOLIO
This hurts. Gimme a hand here. This aggghhhhh—
As Ronnie takes Uncle Malvolio's hand.
Agghhhhhh, Jesus, this is—ohhh, ohhh.
Looking at Ronnie.
Birnbaum, what the hell you doin'?

RONNIE
You says I should hold your hand.
*Tommy returns and sees Uncle Malvolio writhing, Ronnie
crouched beside him.*

TOMMY STONES
What's this? What's goin' on?

UNCLE MALVOLIO
Ohhh, Birnbaum, whata the spooks say?

RONNIE
He's havin' some kind of attack or something.
He tries to pull free, but Uncle Malvolio clings to him.

UNCLE MALVOLIO
The spooks, Birnbaum! Whata they say?

RONNIE
Nothing.

UNCLE MALVOLIO
No, no. Gimme somethin' here!
Then he sags. It's over. He's still. Ronnie straightens up.

TOMMY STONES
Oh, oh, this is bad, this is bad. What happened?
Moving to Uncle Malvolio, trying to find a pulse.

RONNIE
I don't know.

TOMMY STONES
He's dead.

RONNIE
He's dead? Uncle Mal is dead?
Sinking onto the bench.

TOMMY STONES
Now what am I going to do?

RONNIE
He had some kind of attack or something, Tommy.

TOMMY STONES
What am I going to tell them?
Whirling, pacing.

RONNIE
You couldn'da done anything.

TOMMY STONES
Oh, damnit, am I in trouble. Damnit. Damnit!!

RONNIE
It's not your fault.

TOMMY STONES
That's the problem, you moron. I was supposed to whack him, I was supposed to get him outa here!

RONNIE
You was supposed to whack him, Tommy?

TOMMY STONES
Yeah. I took their money and everything. I mean, they gimme the money—no need to name them—these people—you can imagine who they are, what power they fucking wield, and I said I'd take care of it for them, I'd take him out. They'd never have to worry about him again. Now look at this mess.

RONNIE
You said you'd do it. But you didn't—

TOMMY STONES
I can't do it now; look at him. What good would it do?
Lifting Uncle Malvolio's arm, which drops limply.
I can't kill the fuck, he's dead. There would be no point. And I already spent some of their money, the money they paid me. What the hell am I gonna do, Ronnie?

RONNIE
I don't know.
Tommy joins Ronnie on the bench, angrily confronting him as if his problem has somehow been caused by Ronnie.

TOMMY STONES
You're always acting like such a smart-ass, you must have some idea. What am I gonna do?

RONNIE

You could pretend.

TOMMY STONES

I could pretend? I could pretend *what*, Ronnie?

RONNIE

That you done it.

TOMMY STONES

That I done what? Killed him?

RONNIE

Yeah.

TOMMY STONES

You mean I could take credit?

RONNIE

Yeah. Who would know?

TOMMY STONES

I don't know.
> *Getting up, trying to think it through.*

Nobody. Except for you!
> *Suspiciously.*

You would know.

RONNIE

Right. But what am I gonna do—spill the beans? Who would believe me, I said something, anyway? Which I wouldn't.

TOMMY STONES

Right, right, who would believe you?

RONNIE

Nobody. I'm like ridiculous.

TOMMY STONES
Right, right, this is good; I see.
Pacing away, growing excited.
No, no, this is perfect. This is unbelievable. Who would care?

RONNIE
Nobody.

TOMMY STONES
As long as he's dead. That's all they care about. You know who he
reminds me of?

RONNIE
No. Who?
Together they gaze at Uncle Malvolio.

TOMMY STONES
Sittin' there like that. That fuckin' dog.

RONNIE
Oh, yeah?

TOMMY STONES
He was a problem. So this prick was a problem, too. Now they
both got the same fuckin' problem. What happened to that dog,
anyway?

RONNIE
What happened to him, Tommy?

TOMMY STONES
Yeah. I shot him and then . . . ?

RONNIE
Ray . . . put him in the dumpster.
As Tommy follows Ronnie's glance to the dumpster.
You gonna put Uncle Mal in the dumpster? He's awful big.

TOMMY STONES
Ronnie. You think he's got a soul?

RONNIE
What? Who? The dog?

TOMMY STONES
No. You know.
Eyeing Uncle Malvolio.

RONNIE
Him?
They both stare at Uncle Malvolio.

TOMMY STONES
Yeah.

RONNIE
Uncle Mal?

TOMMY STONES
So he's a ghost, you know, this miserable fuckin' ghost stayin' close to home, lurkin' in the shadows. Like Dead Sammy, you were talkin' to him.

RONNIE
You're askin' me?

TOMMY STONES
Who else?
As they both consider Uncle Malvolio.

RONNIE
Maybe.

TOMMY STONES

That would be another kinda problem, I don't even wanna think about it. His miserable soul hangin' around.

He studies Uncle Malvolio.

But you ain't sure.

RONNIE

No.

TOMMY STONES

You know what I'm gonna do.

Pulling strips of rope from his pockets, he starts tying Uncle Malvolio's arms to the wheelchair.

This is what I was planning, I was looking forward to it—I always hated the prick. He actually made me kiss his ass once. In actuality.

Looking at Ronnie.

Don't just sit there. Here!

Tossing hunks of rope to Ronnie.

Tie his feet, tie his legs.

Ronnie obeys, kneeling in front of the wheelchair.

These things are all arranged, you know. They're all arranged. Sometimes by people. Sometimes by whatever. The bosses. He could be a lot of fun, of course, but mainly he was a nasty prick. I guess. But whata I know.

As Ronnie moves back to the bench, Tommy pulls a wad of cash from his pocket.

Here. I want you to take this. It's some of the money.

He places the money in Ronnie's hand.

Now we're in this thing together.

Returning to the wheelchair, he puts Uncle Malvolio's blanket over him, hiding the ropes, tucking in the edges.

I'm gonna wheel him over the river. I am then gonna roll the prick into the river. You wanna come with me? You wanna watch the water close up over him?

RONNIE

No.

TOMMY STONES

It will.

RONNIE

Sure. You're right.

TOMMY STONES

That's what I'm looking forward to. There'll be a splash, some ripples. Bubbles maybe. Then nothin'. It'll all get still. Just the way it was. Not a sign after that. C'mon.

RONNIE

No. I think I'll skip it.

TOMMY STONES

Sure? Suit yourself.
He starts to wheel Uncle Malvolio toward the up right exit.

RONNIE

I think I'll take a rain check.

TOMMY STONES

I wouldn't wanna miss it.

RONNIE

Well, if you missed it, Tommy, who would do it?

TOMMY STONES

Nobody.
He goes, wheeling Uncle Malvolio off.

RONNIE

That's right, Tommy.

> *Calling after Tommy.*

It's up to you.

> *Behind Ronnie, Ray stirs, groans, sits up.*

RAY

Ohhhh, God, what happened?

RONNIE

What?

RAY

My head is killin' me. What happened?

RONNIE

Whata you mean?

RAY

> *Clutching his head.*

My head it's— Ohh, this is brutal.

RONNIE

You drank a lot, Ray.

RAY

I know, my head, my head. I gotta have some aspirin. You got some?

RONNIE

Yeah, sure.

> *Reaching to the paper bag under the bench.*

RAY

Yeah, sure, what?

> *On his knees, Ray watches Ronnie take a bottle of aspirin from the paper bag.*

RAY

You got some aspirin? You really do?

RONNIE
Handing the bottle to Ray.
Yeah, I do.

RAY
Oh, thanks.
Desperately dumping aspirin into his palm.
I need some coffee.

RONNIE
Yeah, sure.
Reaching back into the paper bag.

RAY
You got coffee, too? You really got coffee, too, Ronnie?

RONNIE
Handing a container of coffee to Ray.
Yeah.

RAY
Oh, thank you.

RONNIE
You're welcome.
Ray throws the aspirin into his mouth, drinks the coffee, and stands up.
And . . . Ray.

RAY
What?

RONNIE
Here.
Holding out the money.

RAY
That's money. That's a lot of money.

RONNIE
Yeah. It come to me. It's for the baby.

RAY
Oh. The baby.
He takes the money.

RONNIE
Yeah.

RAY
Thanks.

RONNIE
Sure.

RAY
Ronnie, I gotta go home now to Teresa.
He steps as if to leave.
But before I go, I was wondering—
His eyes go toward the sky.
You ever wish you lived on another planet, Ronnie?

RONNIE
Which one?

RAY
What?

RONNIE
Which one?

RAY
I don't know. I don't know which one. Some other one.

RONNIE
I'd have to know which one.

RAY
Moving back to Ronnie.
You mean like if it was Mars you would say, "No, thanks," but on the other hand Mercury, or maybe Venus might suit you.

RONNIE
Maybe. You gotta be careful.

RAY
Careful? Of what?

RONNIE
There could be worse ones.

RAY
Worse ones? Worse than here?

RONNIE
Sure.

RAY
You really think so?

RONNIE
I'd bet on it.

RAY
Where?

RONNIE
Looking skyward.
Somewhere up there.

RAY
Looking skyward.
Up there?

RONNIE
Still scanning the sky.
Sure. Where else?

They stand looking up; then Ronnie meets Ray's eyes before they both look once more at the sky. Music. Maybe Tony Bennett: "Fly Me to the Moon." Ray looks at the money in his hand, and then he turns and walks off in the fading light. Ronnie sits there, gazing up.

BLACKOUT